Company Commander Training Course:

A Guide for Army Reserve & National Guard Commanders

Charles H. Holmes

www.Part-Time-Commander.com

Legal

Copyright Notice

This book and all related materials are © copyrighted 2018 by Charles Holmes. No part of the contents of this book may be reproduced or transmitted in any form or by any means without permission in writing from the author. Any person who does any unauthorized act in relation to this publication may be liable to criminal prosecution and civil claims for damages.

Disclaimer

Opinions, conclusions and recommendations expressed or implied within are solely those of the author and do not necessarily represent the views to the Department of Defense, Department of the Army, Army National Guard, Army Reserve or any other government agency.

Book Details

Published by Holmes Internet Marketing

ISBN-13: 978-1790926930

Copyright 2018 / All Rights Reserved

Testimonials

Here are some testimonials from some of our happy customers!

"Taking command can be an overwhelming task. Your book helped my quickly gather my thoughts on what tasks I needed to focus on in the first 90 days of taking command. I also use your book to jump start my thoughts on what I need to be tracking on a monthly basis." **Gene H., Current Part-Time Company Commander**

"I found your eBook very helpful. I am a current Company Commander in the Georgia National Guard. After spending five years on active duty with the 101st ABN DIV, the Guard is a unique change and challenge. My husband is a Company Commander on active duty at IBOLC III (IOBC, Ft. Benning) and I suggested that he recommend your book to any of his National Guard Lieutenants. I think it is a great book and suggests many good ways to prioritize the multiple responsibilities and tasks that have to be crammed into two days a month. Great book, very helpful!" **Bridget B., Current Part-Time Company Commander**

"A timely, well organized, no-nonsense book on getting started as a Company Commander, focused on the unique demands of a National Guard officer in this high octane, high OPTEMPO United States Army world; a work that would have saved many a commander a lot of headaches, especially for those who didn't do a proper change-of-command inventory." **Timothy O., former Part-Time Commander**

"As our Guard & Reserve Force are evolving after 10 years of war, I was bothered that there wasn't more on officership for Guard and Reserve leaders. Then I found Chuck's website, and his eBook, 'Part Time Command.' I devoured his experiences and advice and have added it to my leader's kit bag. Many of our FM's and Pubs "forget" about the Guard and focus solely on our active brethren. This eBook is a great addition and helps easily translate active speak into M-Day action plans for M-Day Leaders! Bravo!" **Rus Currie, Captain, ARNG Company Commander**

"Outstanding book! These are the lessons every Company Commander needs, including active duty Army officers. A must read for future and serving Company Commanders. Battalion Commanders would be wise to add this to their officer professional development training." **Jo Rusin, Colonel (ret.) U.S. Army, author of "Women on Your Team: A Man's Guide to Leading Women"**

"A Company Commander has a lot of responsibilities and as a result, he or she must prioritize in order to be effective. After reading the 'Part-Time Company Command eBook' I have a better sense of planning and organizing activities and tasks for mission success. I learned how to address immediate issues that pertained to the development of leaders and Soldiers. I also feel a sense of calm because the eBook can easily be used as a reference guide. I highly recommend the purchase of this book for any new Company Commander." **Ivan O., Company Commander, ILARNG**

"As a part-time (TPU Commander) for a Maintenance Unit, this booked helped in a lot of ways; especially with my command inventories. This book gave me a better understanding of how to conduct an inventory the right way. This eBook helped me throughout my entire command time. It is well detailed from beginning to end." **CW3 Jesus C., Company Commander, PRARNG**

2018 Update

This book was first published in 2009. Originally, it was an eBook. As of December 2018, this is my sixth revision, and hopefully, my final one.

I finished writing the first edition right after I finished Company Command. I've done my best to keep the book updated and relevant.

A lot has happened during the time. I resigned my commission from the National Guard, moved to Florida, and I am now a civilian and full-time blogger. I believe my calling in life is to be a writer.

My website (**www.Part-Time-Commander.com**) has grown into a very popular website, helping officers, NCOs, and soldiers in the USAR and ARNG.

I hope you will take the information you learn in this book and have a successful and enjoyable command experience. Thanks for your service.

Dedication

This book is dedicated to the citizen soldiers who serve their state and nation;

To all former, current and aspiring Company Commanders, and the First Sergeants who help them succeed;

To my former full-time AGR Staff MSG Trimble, SFC Branch, SSG Fitzgerald and SSG Yorkman, I appreciate everything you did to help me succeed as a Company Commander;

To First Sergeant Lewis Wettig, for your leadership and mentorship;

To the officers and NCOs I served with;

To the soldiers in Foxtrot Company, 128th Brigade Support Battalion (Spartans);

And finally, to my beautiful wife, Rachel, for her continuous love and support. I couldn't have done it without you babe.

Hooah!

Table of Contents

Introduction 1

Part One Before You Take Command

1. What it Takes to be an Effective Company Commander 6
2. Managing Your Career Before Company Command 26
3. Applying & Interviewing for a Command Position 38
4. Conducting Your Inventory 46
5. Left-Seat-Right-Seat Ride 50
6. Change-of-Command Ceremony 53

Part Two Your First Year in Command

7. Your First IDT Weekend 57
8. Your First 90 Days 61
9. Working with Your AGR Staff & Command Team 64
10. Balancing Command, Family Time & Life 73
11. Your Typical Monthly Schedule 78

Part Three The Big Things

12. Training Management 82
13. Unit Administration 88
14. Unit Supply 91
15. Unit Maintenance 97
16. Retention 103

17. Physical Fitness 106

18. Family Readiness 110

Part Four Effective Leadership

19. Your Ultimate Purpose 115

20. Establishing Your Priorities 125

21. Effective Time Management 133

22. Developing Leaders 137

23. Soldier Recognition 143

24. Running Meetings 151

Part Five Leaving a Legacy

25. Taking Your Organization to the Next level 158

26. Knowing When to Leave Command 166

27. Life after Company Command 168

Conclusion 170

About the Author 171

Recommended Reading 173

Introduction

Congratulations on your decision to invest in your professional development. It was a wise decision. It is the only investment you can't lose money with.

Reading is the best way to develop your skill-set, both personally and professionally. When you are finished with this book, I know you'll be better prepared to succeed as a part-time Company Commander.

Let me start by introducing myself. My name is Charles Holmes. My friends call me Chuck. I hope you will do the same thing.

I spent 23-months as a Company Commander in the Maryland Army National Guard (2008-2009). I was a traditional M-Day officer, although I did have some prior Active Duty experience.

By military profession, I was a logistician. By trade, I am an entrepreneur. At heart, I'm a no B.S. type of guy.

I'm currently 41 years old and I spent 15+ years serving in the Army, Army Reserve and Army National Guard. I deployed to two combat zones.

I describe myself as humorous, productive and a bit rebellious. Being an enlisted man first, I didn't always fit into the traditional officer mold. I tend to speak my mind, without kissing butt or striving to be politically correct.

Therefore, I might say some things in this book that are contrary to what you've heard throughout your military career. I might even say some things you've thought about, but never had the courage to say.

Everything in this book is my opinion. My views are my own and are in no way endorsed by any government agency. It's my opinion based upon my beliefs, my skill-set, my attitude and my experience.

I don't expect you to or want you to follow me blindly or agree with everything I say. All I ask of you is to keep an open mind and see things from one former Company Commander's viewpoint. I know I can teach you a few things.

Anyway, that's enough about me. **I wrote this book for YOU, not to boast about myself.** If you're wondering why you should read this book, I have an answer for you.

You should read this book because you DESIRE knowledge. You want to be the best Company Commander you can be and you want to learn new things and find new ways to be more effective, efficient and excellent.

If that answer is not good enough, I've got another reason for you. You should read this book because I'm probably one of the only people in the world who spent approximately one thousand hours preparing, drafting, revising and finalizing a book specifically about Company Command in the Army National Guard and Army Reserve.

Sure, there are plenty of books and resources for Active Duty Army Company Commanders. To the best of my knowledge, this is the only book available for part-time Company Commanders.

As a quick reminder, do not get HUNG UP on the phrase "part-time." It is not derogatory or slang. It is simply a buzz-word I use to describe service in the USAR and ARNG.

Before I assumed command, I scoured the Internet, book store and local library to find resources to help me succeed as a Company Commander. I found several books about command, a couple of great websites and some FMs about leadership.

I found nothing specifically geared for National Guard or Army Reserve commanders. When I took command, I made a promise to myself to fill that void. This book evolved from my experience in command.

The book is not an answer to every problem or challenge you will face as a Company Commander. That would be an impossible task.

Instead, this is probably a 90 percent solution to what you need to know to mentally prepare yourself to succeed as a part-time Company Commander.

This book is broken down into five major parts.

- Part One focuses on your time before you take command.
- Part Two focuses on your first year in command.
- Part Three covers "The Big Things."
- Part Four covers "Effective Leadership"
- Part Five discusses "Leaving a Legacy."

Don't just read this book! **STUDY it**. When you read, take your time and take notes. Highlight, underline and use sticky notes.

When you are finished reading the book, share what you learn with your Lieutenants, First Sergeant and peers. Apply what you deem is most important. In three to six months, re-read the book to discover what you missed the first time around. Enjoy!

Part One
Before You Take Command

Chapter 1

What it Takes to be an Effective Company Commander

What does is it take to be an effective Company Commander in the Army National Guard or Army Reserve?

A few things come to mind, but what I think is most important is <u>DESIRE</u>. *If you don't want to be a Company Commander, you shouldn't be one*, even if it's to just check the block so you are eligible for future promotions.

<u>Soldiers deserve competent leaders who WANT to lead them</u>. I'm not saying you will be an effective Company Commander just because you have the desire to be one. However, if you do not have the desire to command troops, YOU CANNOT BE AN EFFECTIVE COMMANDER.

If you've ever served with someone who was a Company Commander, but didn't have the passion to do the job right, you know exactly what I am talking about!

The other traits for being successful in the job are:

- Effective Time Management Skills
- Disciplinc & Confidence
- People Skills
- Excellent Communication Skills
- Big Picture Thinking

- Able & Willing to Make Tough Decisions
- ==Master of Your Emotions==
- Basic Fundamental Technical & Tactical Knowledge
- Leadership

Let's cover each trait in a little more detail.

EFFECTIVE TIME MANAGEMENT SKILLS:

To be effective, you must be able to manage your time effectively. Most M-Day Company Commanders have a family, a civilian day job or business, extra-curricular activities, such as civic club memberships or hobbies, and their M-Day responsibilities.

Compared to your Active Duty counterparts, you have a lot of different things to juggle. From my personal experience, I've found that it's very difficult to manage your time effectively. It can be hard to focus and live your life in balance while in command.

As a part-time Company Commander, you have many "military" responsibilities outside of drill weekend. You have:

- Company Training Meetings
- Battalion Training Meetings
- Inspections
- YTG and YTC Planning Requirements
- Mission Planning for Future Training

- Preparing Reports and Evaluations
- Approving Paperwork
- Counseling and Mentoring
- Inventories
- Site Visits
- And more!

You'll have to find a way to get of all these things done while maintaining a healthy relationship with your spouse and family, AND keeping your civilian employer happy.

That's much easier said than done. To help you manage your time effectively, here are some things you can do:

1) Get a 12-month calendar or day planner from your local office supply store.

2) Review the YTC, YTG and unit training calendar to identify the upcoming training events for the next 12 months.

3) Establish priorities. Determine which events are the most important and require YOU to do to them (i.e. you should lead all company training meetings and attend all battalion training meetings). Add those events to your day planner.

4) Decide which events are less important and empower your AGR and full-time staff to be the tip-of-the-spear. Make sure you leverage your Company XO and First Sergeant, too. Yes, you're still ultimately responsible for everything that needs to get done, but no, you don't need to be the one to physically make everything happen yourself. My rule of

thumb is that if you can delegate it, you should delegate it. Remember the Army pays you to get things done through other people.

5) After you've written down the major military training events in your day planner, and delegated the "less important" tasks to your subordinate leaders, your next step is to schedule in family time, time for your spouse, civilian job responsibilities, time for exercise, your spiritual life, time for your hobbies, etc. Look at your day planner and block off time each day or each week to make sure you have time for these things as well. If you don't schedule it in your day planner, it won't happen. Do NOT neglect your family, spiritual life, or health while in command.

One of the quickest lessons I learned after taking Company Command is that I could be busy, or I could work smart. **Anyone can be busy... and most people are, but effective leaders work smart.**

By following the five steps I just mentioned, I was extremely productive. Remember, we all have 24-hours in a day. It's how you spend your time that matters most.

One more thing...

Company Command will take as much time as you give it (thanks for teaching me that valuable lesson LTC Blair). You must have boundaries and decide what you are willing to do and what you aren't willing to do.

You will never get EVERYTHING done, especially if you try to do it all yourself. You must empower others, set boundaries, have office hours, set priorities and keep the main thing the main thing.

Otherwise, your command responsibilities will take over your life. That's fine if you are serving in the Active Duty Army, but that won't work if you have a civilian day job and family.

You really can manage your day job, command time and family time if you are good with time management. Decide from day one how MUCH time you will invest in your command each week and have the discipline to come up with a schedule and follow it.

DISCIPLINE & CONFIDENCE:

As a Company Commander, you're the top of the food chain within your unit. As Army officers, our soldiers look to us to be confident and poised. When the bullets start flying or the shit hits the fan, that's when you need to be at your best.

In addition, *Soldiers want discipline*. Many of them joined the Army for the discipline. ==Your job is to set the standards high and to enforce the standards equally to everyone under your authority==.

Soldiers do not want a wishy-washy, weak Company Commander. They want someone they can respect; someone they can admire, and someone who is ==firm, fair and consistent==.

In addition, **you must act confident**. When you talk with someone, look them in the eye. Don't slouch when you walk.

Suck in your gut, straighten up your shoulders, tighten your chin strap, and walk with your head held high. Believe in yourself and your abilities.

<u>Don't be arrogant though</u>. Don't act as if you are better than everyone else. Don't act like your shit don't stink. My best advice is to **be calm, cool and collected!**

If you have confidence or worthiness issues, get some help. Read some books about confidence, personal power, and developing a positive mental attitude and/or talk to the Chaplain or a psychologist if needed.

Soldiers deserve a confident and disciplined leader.

Here are a few discipline tips I can share with you that worked well for me:

- Always set a strong personal example (lead from the front)
- Never ask your soldiers to do something that you wouldn't do yourself
- Make sure everyone under your command knows the standards
- <u>Enforce the standards to everyone equally</u>
- Be confident in your own abilities (but not arrogant)
- Don't be scared to make a decision
- Don't keep changing your mind or be indecisive
- Do what you say you are going to do
- *Don't try to be your soldiers' friend or buddy*

PEOPLE SKILLS:

To be effective as a Company Commander, you must develop excellent people skills. Don't forget that most of your soldiers are civilians 28-days a month.

Treat everyone with respect. <u>Utilize the Golden Rule and treat people the way you want to be treated.</u> Yes, there is a rank structure, but we are all people, too.

Soldiers will go the extra mile for the leader they trust and respect.

To get the most out of your team, learn things about each person you lead. Learn their personality type. Find out their goals, natural talents and abilities. Find out what they are good at and focus on that.

Realize that each of your followers is motivated differently and wired differently. For instance, some soldiers enjoy being recognized in front of the entire unit, but others HATE public recognition.

Some people are extroverts while other people are introverts. Some people are self-motivated and ambitious, while others aren't.

Find out what makes each one of your people tick. Get a notepad and take notes. Write down the important things about your soldiers. Information such as spouse's or children's names, birthdays, hobbies and interests will be very helpful.

As a quick reminder, you're not trying to be your soldiers' friend. You want to keep clear boundaries and not try to be buddy-buddy with your soldiers, but you can really improve the "output" of your soldiers by showing them that you care about them.

One more thing... **People rise to the expectations that we place on them.** If you expect greatness out of your people, most of them will step up to the plate and act great.

On the other hand, if you think of each person on your team as a slacker, or someone who is worthless, that is how they will act. Always expect greatness out of everyone you lead. Demand it!

If you would like to improve your people skills, I suggest you read the book "How to Win Friends and Influence People" by Dale Carnegie. That book helped me a lot.

COMMUNICATION SKILLS:

Do you know why most couples argue and fight? The answer is poor communication.

Do you know why communication gets distorted within most organizations? Because information does not flow downward properly! That's assuming the information actually gets disseminated to the lowest levels in the first place.

As the Company Commander, you must be able to effectively articulate your vision to your soldiers. You must ensure that "what they are hearing" corresponds with "what you are saying."

Everyone MUST understand your message and intent. This includes verbal and non-verbal communication.

One way to improve communication is to give your message to your entire company at the same time, not just your direct reports. If you have important information, share it with the entire company at once.

Use a newsletter. Use a message board. Send an important email to everyone in the unit. Use a dry erase board or butcher's block in the common area of your unit.

Send a copy of the OPORD to everyone. Have a company formation and tell everyone what is on your mind.

In addition, you must develop effective "public speaking" skills. More often than not, you will speak to your soldiers as one entity, either in formation or in a classroom environment. When you are speaking, you MUST appear confident, even if you're not. Get rid of the "ums" and "ahs."

One thing that really helped my communication skills was enrolling in *Toastmasters* two years before I took Company Command. It improved my confidence and taught me how to communicate effectively in front of an audience. You might want to check out Toastmasters. It's time and money well spent.

One of my biggest challenges as a Company Commander was communication distortion.

In other words, by the time my messages were filtered from my Platoon Leaders all the way down to the soldier level, the messages were often inaccurate.

Some techniques I used to overcome that problem were:

- Publishing a Monthly Newsletter
- Posting information on the Unit Bulletin Board

- Issuing OPORDs to the entire company as a whole, not just PLs

- Conducting Back Briefs with PLs, PSGs and First Line Leaders

- Randomly "spot checking" soldiers to see if they knew the mission statement and commander's intent

- Writing my intent and priorities on a dry erase board located in the common area

I found these methods very helpful. The bottom line is to work on your communication skills.

BIG PICTURE THINKING

As the Company Commander **you get paid to think about the big picture.** This includes the vision, strategy, and future of your organization. Your job is similar to the role of the CEO in a traditional business.

That means you have to be able to separate the minutia from the important stuff. You have to be able to look out into the future and set a vision for what you want your organization to look like.

You have to be able to step back from everything that needs to be done right now and ask yourself WHY you are doing it and how will it affect your organization as an entity.

One of my best leadership tips I learned from a businessman. His name is Michael Gerber and he is the author of the best-selling book "The E-Myth Revisited." In that book he talks about the difference between successful entrepreneurs and failing entrepreneurs.

He claims that successful entrepreneurs work "on" their business, while failing entrepreneurs work "in" their business. I think you should do the same thing during your time in command.

Work on your organization... **Let your 1SG, NCOs and Platoon Leaders work in the organization while you work on it**. This is the primary and most important responsibility of the head of an organization.

To me, this lesson alone is worth THOUSANDS of dollars, hundreds of hours, and reduced frustration. If you get nothing else from this book adopt this mindset into your leadership style.

Always focus on the big picture. Big Picture Thinking includes:

- Planning for future missions
- Developing strategy
- Looking for areas of improvement in your organization
- Sharing your vision with your subordinate leaders and soldiers
- Looking at your unit from the outside in rather than the inside out
- Establishing best practices, policies and procedures
- Growing people
- Setting short-term and long-term goals for your organization

- Asking yourself "WHY" am I doing what I am doing

<u>At the company level, it's easy to forget about the big picture.</u> You have so many last-minute deadlines and unexpected fires to put out.

You can have a perfect plan for drill weekend, but by the time you show up at the armory, everything changes. Unexpected meetings, suspenses, deadlines, training events, and guidelines come down from higher headquarters and mess up your plan.

Sometimes it feels like you are trying to put ten pounds of stuff into a five-pound bag.

During drill weekend, I spent about 40 percent of my time working on Big Picture Thinking and about 60 percent of my time putting out fires (day-to-day deals). Looking back, I should have spent about 80 percent of my time on Big Picture Thinking and 20 percent of my time putting out fires.

Learn from my experience and don't make the same mistake I did. Let your XO and command team handle those things. That is what they get paid to do. Fortunately, I worked on the "big picture thinking" outside of drill weekend on my own time, so my unit was very successful.

Empower your full-time AGR Staff, NCOs, Platoon Leaders and command team to take care of most of the day-to-day details, but have them keep you informed on the major issues.

Remember, your job is to work on the big things, not to take care of every little issue that comes up.

As the head of the organization, you have a responsibility to create the vision for the organization, to establish best practices and policies, to look for ways to improve the unit, to grow people, to ensure all mission requirements are complete, and to serve as a liaison between your battalion and your company.

Don't ever forget that. At least once a week, you should pause for a minute or two and reflect on the past week.

How did you spend your time? Were you effective? What could you have done differently to work smarter? What did you do that you shouldn't be doing? What DIDN'T you do that you should be doing?

Your job as the leader is to determine where you want your organization to go. You are the Captain of the ship. *You determine the destination, but your team will take care of the details to make sure you arrive at the right place, and on time!*

As a final point, remember this: **you are future operations while your 1SG and AGR Staff are current operations**. You should always focus on 30, 60 and 90 days out (and longer).

ABLE & WILLING TO MAKE TOUGH DECISIONS:

I'm going to be straight forward with this one. You will face tough situations where you need to make a difficult decision, sometimes in a matter of seconds. What will separate you from being effective or ineffective is your ability to make the decision.

Most of the decisions you have to make could be made by a third grader. However, **you get paid the big bucks**

because of the FEW, yet TOUGH decisions you have to make. Some of the tough decisions you might be faced with include:

- Dealing with poor performance
- Having to write a bad evaluation report for someone
- Reductions & demotions
- Deciding whether you will enforce the Army standard to EVERYONE in your unit
- Initiating discharge or transfer paperwork for a bad Soldier
- Making a war-time decision that could affect someone's life

When possible, collect the facts, verify the first report, listen to both sides of the story, and then follow your intuition and make a decision.

If time permits, and you need to counsel with your First Sergeant, Battalion Commander, JAG or Chaplain first, by all means get their input.

But once you get the facts, make a decision. One of the things soldiers hate the most is a leader who can't make a decision. The second thing they hate is a leader who changes their mind all the time.

Be quick to make a decision and slow to change it.

Don't be slow to make a decision and quick to change it.

Remember, you are the leader. You are the decision maker. **Don't ask your boss for permission to make decisions.** That's what the Army pays you to do!

Also, there will be times when you make the WRONG decision. It happens. You're human. <mark>When you are wrong, admit it</mark>.

Let your team know you made a mistake, what you learned from it, and how you will fix things. Your team will respect you for doing that.

MASTER OF YOUR EMOTIONS

Earlier in this chapter, I mentioned the importance of being confident and poised. As humans, <u>we are emotional creatures</u>. Sometimes our emotions can get the best of us.

This is something I am constantly aware of with myself. I'm naturally an emotional guy and I have to work really hard at keeping my emotions balanced.

The Company Commander needs to be the MASTER of their emotions. That means having <u>SELF-CONTROL</u>. It means thinking before you speak. It means, getting the facts, before you speculate or make irrational decisions.

If you get frustrated, discouraged, disappointed or upset, that's fine. Just don't let your soldiers see you that way. Take five minutes, go into your office, do what you need do to calm down and then come back out with your game-face on.

<mark>*If you filter your frustrations downwards, you have failed as a leader.*</mark> Remember, <u>problems go up, not down</u>. Your soldiers have enough to worry about. They don't need to worry about your troubles, too.

Whenever possible, stay calm, cool and collected!

Remember that **you are the thermostat in your unit.** Your emotions, poise and confidence will be "passed on" to others in your unit. Make sure you are setting a good example.

BASIC FUNDAMENTAL TECHNICAL & TACTICAL KNOWLEDGE

Company Commanders are the senior trainers in their companies. The First Sergeant handles individual training, but you are responsible for the collective training.

You must have basic fundamental knowledge about Army tactics and you must have a thorough understanding of your officer branch and the technical and tactical missions of your unit.

If you command a company different from your basic branch, or are in a command designated branch immaterial, you must spend some time familiarizing yourself with the terms, acronyms and missions of your unit <u>BEFORE</u> you take command.

Read the relevant FMs. Talk with other officers. Whatever you do, get your shit together. In the heat of the battle, your Soldiers will rely on you to plan the mission and take care of them.

If you don't have basic fundamental knowledge about tactics and your officer branch, do yourself a favor and acquire it before you even apply for a command position.

<u>This is the primary reason you should NOT be in a rush to take command</u>. You need EXPERIENCE. You need on the job training.

To gain this knowledge, read every FM and regulation you can find that applies to your unit.

Study Army Operations. Read your unit's ARTEP. Take a class on tactics. Learn everything you can from your NCOs. Do whatever it takes to gain this knowledge.

LEADERSHIP

Leadership is an art-form. Just because you are an Army officer doesn't make you a leader. You have to earn that title by your actions.

To me, a leader is someone with influence, who can get the job done, and who can rally others to support their cause. A leader is a person that others respect and admire and want to follow!

Leadership is LEARNED and EARNED. No one starts out as a leader. No one is born a leader.

If you are doing the other things I talked about in this chapter, you will be well on your way to be an effective military leader and Company Commander.

I didn't really hit my leadership stride until I became a Captain, so if your leadership skills aren't up to par yet, don't fret.

That being said, there are a few leadership qualities you should develop before you take command. Here are a few things that come to mind when I think of great leaders:

Vision – Seeing the big picture and seeing things before they exist

Influence – Having people who want to follow you

<u>Honesty</u> – Doing what you say you will do and being a person of your word

<u>Integrity</u> – Doing the right thing at all times

<u>Respect</u> – Respecting the people you lead and work with as individuals

<u>Confidence</u> – Believing in yourself and your own abilities

<u>Followership</u> – Good leaders are also good followers

<u>Un-selfishness</u> - Being a team-player and putting the unit, mission & others first

<u>Caring</u> – Caring about the people that you lead as people

Do everything you can do to fine tune and improve your leadership skills before you take command.

One of my favorite leadership books of all time is ==“The 21 Irrefutable Laws of Leadership”== by Dr. John Maxwell. Order a copy of that book and read it!

SUMMARY

In summary, Company Commanders are expected to be the tip-of-the-spear in their units.

Even though you might only be 25 to 30-years old, you're expected to be the leader, the expert, the coach, the mentor, the father/mother, etc.

To be an effective, efficient and excellent Company Commander you should at a minimum, have these basic attributes:

- Desire to Command & Lead Troops

- Effective Time Management Skills
- Discipline & Confidence
- People Skills
- Excellent Communication Skills
- Big Picture Thinking
- Able & Willing to Make Tough Decisions
- Master of Your Emotions
- Basic Fundamental Technical & Tactical Knowledge
- Leadership Skills

It would be a wise decision to spend fifteen to thirty minutes right now and assess where you currently stand in each one of these areas.

Obviously, you will have strengths and weaknesses. That's okay. Everyone does. Just take some time and identify areas that you can improve upon.

Once you know your shortcomings, come up with an action plan to help you improve each area.

Some of the quickest ways to do that include:

- Read books
- Study the FMs
- Take a class
- Find a mentor

Remember, <u>you are a work in progress</u>. No one is perfect. We all have shortcomings. However, if you simply strive to get a little bit better each day, you can become a dynamic leader in a short amount of time.

Chapter 2

Managing Your Career Before Company Command

Many young officers make the mistake of jumping into Company Command as quickly as possible. In my opinion, that's one of the biggest career mistakes you can make.

I've watched numerous officers assume command as a junior or senior First Lieutenant. <u>Most of these officers have struggled to be effective commanders</u>.

To be a successful Company Commander, you need experience, wisdom and maturity. You acquire these three assets through life experience and military experience.

Unfortunately, as a Second Lieutenant or First Lieutenant or even a young Captain you don't have too much wisdom or maturity.

At 25-30 years old, you don't have very much life experience or military experience, either. It's important to remember that an Army Reserve or National Guard Officer has less military experience than their Active Duty counterpart.

In essence 3-4 years in the National Guard is about the same amount of <u>military</u> experience as one year of Active Duty experience.

On the flip side of the coin, National Guard and Army Reserve officers have civilian/corporate experience that is extremely valuable.

In reality, they probably do something different in their civilian job than they do as a military officer. This makes them well rounded.

Remember this; **Company Command should be the culmination of your junior officer development, not the first step.**

In other words, you should have several different Army jobs prior to taking Company Command.

In my opinion, you should spend time as a Platoon leader, Company XO and Battalion Staff Officer prior to taking command.

These jobs will help you establish a solid leadership foundation and will teach you the skills and knowledge required to be a successful Company Commander.

Let's take a few moments and review what you'll learn in each one of these jobs.

WHAT YOU'LL LEARN AS A PLATOON LEADER:

Most new Lieutenants begin their military careers as Platoon Leaders. As a Platoon Leader, you will establish your leadership foundation.

You'll get to spend 9 to 18-months working with a senior NCO, probably a Sergeant First Class. They will teach you what "right" looks like; hopefully.

In addition, you will lead between 20 and 50 soldiers depending upon what type of platoon you are assigned to. You'll learn the ropes about training, time-management, decision making, counseling, discipline, meetings and much more.

Your primary goal as a Platoon Leader is to learn the basics about the Army and learn how to lead soldiers. You'll also develop your own management and leadership style, based upon your personality, strengths and weaknesses, and experience.

You'll deal with discipline issues, soldier issues and get experience drafting OPORDs. You will attend company training meetings and host your own platoon meetings.

You will also learn about collective training, METL development and much more.

Once you have completed 9-18 months as a Platoon Leader, you should have a clear perspective about your own personal leadership style, how a platoon operates within a company, and how things work in the military.

At this point, you should seek out a position as a Company Executive Officer.

WHAT YOU'LL LEARN AS A COMPANY EXECUTIVE OFFICER:

After spending 9 to 18-months as a Platoon Leader, your next leadership position should be as a Company Executive Officer (XO). Serving as a Company XO is an awesome job. It was my favorite job in the Army.

As the Company XO, you will run the day-to-day operations of the unit, along with the First Sergeant. Your primary responsibility will be to assist the commander in areas such as administration, supply and maintenance.

You'll gain valuable experience working with the Supply Sergeant. You will learn about Physical Security and the Command Supply Discipline Program.

You'll also learn about inventories and property accountability. This will really help you out when you are preparing to take Company Command, a few years down the road.

In addition, you'll also get experience with administration. This could include writing NCOERs, OERs and awards. You'll also oversee promotions, separations, schools, pay problems and so much more.

Next, you'll get some experience working in the Motor Pool. You'll learn about Maintenance Reports, such as the 026, how to order parts, how to PMCS a vehicle, HAZMAT and so much more.

You will manage the company maintenance program, along with the Motor Sergeant. You will ensure your equipment is maintained, accounted for and ready to deploy.

Other benefits include running meetings, serving as the acting Commander (when the Company Commander is absent) and mentoring the Platoon Leaders.

If possible, you should spend 9 to 12-months as a Company XO.

By the time you are finished your time as a Company XO, you should clearly understand how platoons operate within a company, and the role of the company staff.

In addition, you will have some experience with company and battalion operations. You should have a better understanding how companies operate within a battalion.

Once your Company XO time is up, you should be eligible for Captain. You'll have about 36 to 42-months' time in service. At this point, you should actively seek out a primary Battalion Staff Officer position.

WHAT YOU'LL LEARN AS A BATTALION STAFF OFFICER:

Once you finish your time as a Company XO, you should find a position on the Battalion Staff. As a Battalion Staff Officer, you will learn how a battalion functions.

More importantly, you will learn how "companies" operate within the battalion and how battalions operate within a brigade. Let's just call it, the "big picture."

You could serve as a S1 (Adjutant), S2 (Intel), S4 (Logistics), S6 (Signal) or Assistant S3. Typically, S3 positions are reserved for Majors or senior Captains who have already commanded.

However, there are sometimes exceptions to this rule.

As a Battalion Staff Officer, you will coordinate, plan and resource with the brigade, battalion and companies. You will ensure the companies are in compliance with battalion objectives, and ensure the battalion is in compliance with brigade objectives.

In addition, you will ensure the companies are staffed and resourced to complete their missions.

You will also get experience with the Military Decision Making Process, something that will help you a lot as a Company Commander.

You should spend somewhere between 9 to 18-months on staff. This will give you enough exposure to your battalion.

When your staff time is finished, if possible, you should try to get a command position within the same battalion.

The reason you will want to do this is you will have a complex understanding of how your battalion operates. Plus, you should have a good network of relationships with the Battalion Commander, Battalion XO, and the other Company Commanders.

Staff Officers generally don't get very much credit. Overall, staff officers are a dime-a-dozen, but a great staff officer is a rare breed.

As an Army officer, most of your career will be as a staff officer. If you have a successful 20-year career, you will spend about 4 to 6-years in command and the other 14 to 16-years on staff. With that in mind, you should strive to be an excellent staff officer.

WHAT IF I HAVEN'T HAD THESE POSITIONS, BEFORE I TAKE COMMAND?

First of all, don't worry. Typically, you have little say about which unit will be your first assignment.

You'll be placed where there are Army officer shortages for your specific branch.

Just because you don't have all of these duty positions before you take Company Command does not mean you won't be ready or qualified to be a Company Commander.

Although these are the best developmental jobs for command, as I see it, other jobs can be beneficial, too. Other beneficial jobs could include Aide-de-Camp, Assistant Brigade Staff, Instructor, or TAC Officer.

These jobs are usually filled by Senior Captains, but are sometimes filled with Lieutenants or junior Captains.

Remember this; <u>you're only a Lieutenant and junior Captain once</u>. As a Lieutenant and Captain, more than any other rank, you will have the MOST exposure working closely with soldiers. I call it "troop time."

"Troop time" is very important. <u>VERY IMPORTANT</u>. **Working closely with troops will be the most beneficial leadership development time you will have in the Army.**

I would suggest you spend your entire junior officer time at the company level, in a line unit, because after Company Command you will spend most of your career on staff, away from the troops.

In addition, you will never get a second chance to build a strong leadership foundation.

The best advice I can give you is this. <u>Manage your own career</u>. Don't just take a job because that's what you're offered. Know what jobs you need to take in order to continue your professional development. Once you know what job you need, SEEK that job out.

Leaders respect junior officers who are squared away, self-motivated and have a game-plan for their own career. If you're good at what you do, chances are your supervisor will be very supportive and respect the fact that you are ACTIVELY managing your own career.

On the other hand, if for some reason you cannot land the job you are seeking, that's okay. Whatever job you get, take pride in what you do and be the best you possibly can be.

Remember, *the job doesn't make the person, the person makes the job.* Whatever you are, be great at it! People will notice.

Your Civilian & Military Education...

YOUR BACHELOR'S DEGREE:

Most Army officers already have a Bachelor's degree, before they are commissioned. That puts them slightly ahead of Army officers who don't have a 4-year degree yet.

If you don't already have a Bachelor's degree, <u>GET ONE QUICKLY</u>! As you probably know, Lieutenants cannot get promoted to Captain without a Bachelor's degree from a regionally accredited college or university.

There are few things more disappointing than seeing a squared away officer STUCK at the First Lieutenant rank because they do not have their degree yet.

I've even seen some officers lose their officer status and be demoted to E-5 because they did not finish their college degree in time. If you don't have a college degree yet, your top priority should be acquiring one.

Visit your local Military Education Office to learn more about different degree programs via online and/or traditional methods. If you don't get your degree within the designated time-frame the Army allows, you can be separated from the Army.

Why throw away your career if you don't have to? Finish your degree!

YOUR MASTER'S DEGREE:

Obtaining a Master's Degree is a quick way to separate yourself from your peers.

Although having a Master's Degree is not required for promotion to the rank of Captain, it doesn't hurt your cause.

There's no perfect time in your career to acquire a Master's Degree. In my opinion, the earlier you complete the degree, the better off you will be.

As you move up through the ranks, and with your family and professional career, you will continue to have increased responsibilities. *You will be busier and have less time.*

I personally acquired my Master's Degree as a young First Lieutenant. It was painful and time consuming, but well worth it. To learn more about Master's Degree programs, visit your military education office or search online.

YOUR MILITARY EDUCATION:

The Army wants officers with a solid civilian and military education. As a result, the Army created what is known as OES or Officer Educational System.

According to AR 350-1, para. 3-23 (dated 3 August 2007):

"The goal of the OES is to produce a corps of leaders who are fully competent in technical, tactical and leadership skills, knowledge and experience; are knowledgeable of how the Army runs; are prepared to operate in joint, integrated, and multinational environments; demonstrate confidence, integrity, critical judgment, and responsibility; can operate in an environment of complexity, ambiguity, and rapid change; can build effective teams amid organizational and technological change; and can adapt to and solve problems creatively.

The OES prepares commissioned officers for increased responsibilities and successful performance at the next higher level.

It provides pre-commissioning, branch, functional area, and leader–development training that prepares officers to lead platoon, company, battalion and higher-level organizations.

The OES consists of branch–immaterial and branch–specific courses that provide progressive and sequential training throughout an officer's career. Regardless of branch affiliation, functional area, or specialty, the common thread, which ties all OES courses together, is common–core training. Common core training is approved by TRADOC and incorporated into OES courses."

WHAT COURSES DO YOU NEED?

It is my belief that you should complete your Basic Officer Leadership Course (BOLC), the Captain's Career Course (CCC) and Pre-Command Course prior to taking command.

BOLC teaches Lieutenants about Army tactics, military customs and courtesies, leadership principles, and general knowledge about their officer branch.

The CCC teaches senior First Lieutenants and Captains branch specific information and branch-immaterial staff process training. Simply put, they teach Captains how to function on the battalion and brigade level staff.

Most units require Captains to complete the Pre-Command Course before they can command a unit.

The Pre-Command Course teaches you about Yearly Training Calendars, Yearly Training Guidance, After Action Reviews, legal considerations, Equal Opportunity, and much more. I found it to be a very helpful course.

Another thing to consider is that some schools are required for promotion. In accordance with AR 135-155, Table 2-2 dated 13 July 2004, you MUST complete BOLC prior to promotion to Captain.

The Captain's Career Course is required for Captains to be promoted to the rank of Major.

I've found that the sooner you can complete your military education, the better. Completing your military education requirements ahead of schedule is a huge key to success.

As an Army Reserve or National Guard Officer, you are expected to complete the same military education requirements as an Active Duty officer.

Although many of your courses are non-resident (online distance learning), compared to the Active Duty resident courses, you'll still get a similar education.

I've seen countless Army officers FAIL to get promoted because they did not complete their military education requirements. They procrastinated and did not manage their own career the right way.

Don't let that happen to you. If you have officers under your authority, don't let that happen to them either.

THE BOTTOM LINE

The bottom line is to complete your military and civilian education requirements ahead of time and make sure you have the right jobs before you take command. This will give you the experience and knowledge to be a successful commander.

Chapter 3

Applying & Interviewing for a Command Position

Once you've decided that you're ready to serve as a Company Commander, you need to do three things.

They are:

1) Find a vacant Company Command position

2) Complete your application packet and formally apply for the position

3) Interview for the position

Let's cover each one of these things in greater detail.

FIND A VACANT COMPANY COMMAND POSITION:

There are several different ways to find vacant Company Command positions in your state. You can utilize your "network" and ask around. Talk with your peers, friends and mentors to learn about vacancies and upcoming opportunities.

The best way to find out about potential or future openings is to talk with current Company Commanders who have been in command for a while (18-months or more) and will be leaving command in a few months. This can give you insider information that hasn't been posted yet.

Next, you can also search the state's website on your own, or sit down with your Battalion S1 Officer. You can search for postings on the position vacancies page. You can also do a search in SIDPERS by rank and branch to see the vacancies within your state.

There's another important consideration here.

<u>Depending on your state, you may not have the opportunity to command within your specific branch.</u>

For instance, if you are a Chemical Corps Officer, and your state does not have a Chemical Company, you will need to find a command that is branch immaterial.

That's okay. Command is command (for the most part). *When possible, you should try to command within your branch, in an operational unit.* <u>You want to command a deployable, go-to-war unit.</u>

Why? Because that is what the Army is all about. If I had to choose between a deployable, MTOE unit or a TDA, non-deployable unit, I would pick the MTOE unit every time. Trust me, it's better for career progression.

If that's not possible, find the best opportunity available and make the most of it. If you are good at what you do, you will get noticed, regardless of what type of company you command.

The secret to success, and to get the company you want, is to be proactive. If you cannot find the command you want within your own state, but you know of an opening in a bordering state, you may consider doing an inter-state transfer to get the command you want.

Remember, it's your job to manage your career. You might have to make a temporary sacrifice to reach your long-term goals.

There is one last question to ask yourself. What unit should I command? There are two answers to this question.

Number one, which unit appeals to you the most and would be the most enjoyable to command? Is there a unit that you really love? Is there a unit that would be your dream command? If so, pursue it.

The next answer is worth considering.

One of the best pieces of career advice I ever received was to look for the most JACKED UP unit you could find. Say, what?

Look for the unit that has horrible morale, retention issues, and countless other problems. Look for the most incompetent Company Commander in the state and be their replacement.

WHY? *Because when you replace a bad Company Commander, or take over a shitty unit, you have nowhere to go but up!* Never forget that advice.

When you take over the best unit around, you have nowhere to go but down. When you replace a Company Commander who was at the top of his/her game, the best of the best, you have nowhere to go but down. But, when you take over a crappy unit, and you are a good leader, you will become a hero!

This is really valuable information to consider. I wish someone would have shared this information with me when I was a young officer.

COMPLETE YOUR APPLICATION PACKET AND FORMALLY APPLY:

Once you've identified a command vacancy for which you want to apply for, your next step is to start building your packet.

Typically, the following documents are required in a command packet:

- Current 2-1
- Current DA Photo
- Last 3 OERs
- Current HT/WT and APFT Info
- Letters of Recommendation

You should already have most of these documents in your "I Love Me Book." If not, spend a couple hours and update it. It's important to always have these documents at your disposal.

Now, you need to review each document to check for accuracy.

Is your DA Photo current? If you've received an award or got promoted since your last photo, you should get your photo updated ASAP. When possible, try to have a DA photo taken within 90-days of applying for the command position. This shows the interviewers that you are proactive.

Is your DA 2-1 current? More importantly, is it accurate? When was it last updated? Are all of your past jobs reflected on it? If not, visit your PSB Office or Battalion S1 and get it fixed ASAP.

How about your APFT and HT/WT information? Are they current? Did you pass the APFT and HT/WT? Is your score the best it could possibly be? If it's outdated or inaccurate, get with your unit and retake the APFT.

Redo your HT/WT too. Try to have an APFT score above 270 and take an APFT within 60-days of applying for the position.

How about Letters of Recommendation? Do you have Letters of Recommendation from your previous supervisor or Battalion Commander? If you were an Aide-de-Camp, do you have a LOR from the General? If not, get one.

I suggest you try to assemble at least three different Letters of Recommendation. *Have the person writing the LOR discuss how your skills and experience prepare you for the command position you are applying for.* This will make a big difference.

Another thing you should do is draft up a Memorandum for Record to the President of the Selection Board (normally the Battalion Commander). Talk about your desire to take command of that specific unit and review your previous experience and explain how it pertains to this duty position. This is one additional way to separate yourself from your peers.

Everything we just reviewed sounds like common sense. However, many National Guard and Army Reserve officers let these things slack. Do not be a slacker. Separate yourself from your competition by doing a little bit extra.

Besides, when the Colonel and the selection board review your packet, they are going to check these documents anyway. Set yourself up for success, before you even enter the actual interview. It will only help your cause.

INTERVIEW FOR THE POSITION:

Interviewing is a science. The secret to a successful interview is preparation. You should do your due diligence before the interview. Spend several hours learning about the unit mission and the unit history. Learn the structure of the unit.

Study the MTOE to learn more about personnel and equipment authorization levels. Get a copy of the unit training schedule and Battalion YTC, ahead of time. Identify upcoming training events. Also, check out the battalion mission statement, Yearly Training Calendar and battalion history.

If you are really motivated, you should try to learn a little bit about each person on the interview board. If you do nothing else, take the outgoing Company Commander out to lunch or simply give them a call a few weeks before the interview. Get to know them a little bit. Express your interest in their job.

Find out the strengths and weaknesses of the unit. Ask them any questions you might have. This information will be very helpful. Do this right and they will "sell" the other interviewers on the board about why they should pick you.

On the day of the interview, prep your uniform and have a "buddy" or your spouse check it too.

Get a fresh haircut and by all means, make sure your breath is fresh. Arrive to the interview five to ten minutes early. Don't get there too early, and don't you dare be late.

When you are told to report, knock three times and ask for permission to enter. During the interview, try to stay calm and relaxed. Smile. Maintain good eye contact with the interviewers. Lean forward in your seat. Check your attitude.

Be polite and respectful to everyone in the room. Answer all of their questions to the best of your ability and appear CONFIDENT. If you don't know the answer, simply state so, and tell them that you will get back to them with the answer.

You probably won't know exactly what questions they are going to ask you ahead of time. Some of the most common interview questions include:

1. Why would you be the right person for the job?
2. What separates you from the other people competing for the job?
3. What do you know about the unit?
4. What would you do in your first 90-days?
5. What is your leadership style?
6. What job experience do you have that makes you qualified for the job?
7. Why do you want to be the commander?

If you've done your prep work, you'll be fine.

At a minimum, be familiar with the MTOE, personnel, mission and history of the unit.

One thing you can do to help your cause is ask a few of your Company Commander peers what type of questions they were asked during their command interview.

Remember, **your goal is to create a favorable and lasting impression**. When you leave the interview, you want the interviewers to say "that officer is squared away" or "she obviously prepared for this meeting."

Be sure you put your best foot forward. I think you'll be quite surprised how many applicants "half ass" it. Always go the extra mile.

One last tip. Finish the interview strong. At the end of the interview, take 30 to 90-seconds to summarize WHY they should choose you for the job over everyone else. This will let you leave the interview on a favorable impression.

GETTING SELECTED OR REJECTED FOR COMMAND:

You've finished the interview process. You feel confident about your interview. What's going to happen now? One of two things will happen: you'll either get selected for the position or you won't.

Guess what? You never really know what will happen. If you were prepared, you should expect to be selected for the job.

Also, if you were the only applicant, you have even better chances. However, if you don't get selected for the position, don't worry.

Everything happens for a reason. This "rejection" could turn out to be the biggest blessing in your life.

If you are rejected for the position, take a couple days to reflect on the experience. If you still have the desire to command, look for another unit and start the process all over again.

If you get a "selection letter" in the mail, congratulations. You're ready to move forward to the next step: conducting your inventory.

Chapter 4

Conducting Your Inventory

Before you actually take command, you must conduct a "change-of-command inventory" to properly accept accountability and responsibility for the unit's equipment.

This one task can set you up for success or failure, right from the start.

One of the greatest bits of advice I can give you is to prepare, be thorough and <u>DO NOT</u> sign any documents until you are 100% sure they are accurate.

In other words, don't sign for items you have not physically identified, touched and inventoried.

How do you prepare for a change-of-command-inventory? Here is what I suggest you do.

<u>As the Incoming Company Commander, you should:</u>

1. Educate yourself about Army inventories. Read different manuals, have the Supply Sergeant give you a block of instruction about inventories, and talk with former Company Commanders to get any tips you can from them. Tag along with another commander in a different unit when they are doing an inventory (of any kind) and take notes.

2. Visit with Battalion Commander and Property Book Officer to get guidance prior to the start of the inventory. Verify the master inventory packet compiled by the outgoing commander to ensure it is complete.

Review DA Pam 25-30 to ensure the most current publications are available. If no publication is available an inventory list will be created to account for components.

3. Compare the property book against the sub-hand receipts to ensure all unit property is sub-hand receipted to the end user. Identify any equipment loaned outside of the unit to ensure it's on a valid hand receipt.

4. Conduct a 100% inventory of the unit's property and report any discrepancies to the outgoing commander for resolution. Verify that all discrepancies are corrected prior to assuming responsibility. You have 30-days to conduct the inventory and if needed, you can get one 15-day extension.

5. Once all discrepancies are resolved sign the new hand receipt acknowledging responsibility for the property.

That's how things are supposed to work. Remember, as a traditional Army Reserve or National Guard Company Commander, you have the same amount of time to conduct your inventory that an Active Duty Company Commander has.

Obviously, you have job and family commitments outside of the military. You probably can't afford to take 30-days off from your job to conduct the inventory. That's okay.

Your secret to success is to ensure the outgoing Company Commander and Supply Sergeant have prepared for the inventory.

If they conduct a pre-change-of-command inventory like they are supposed to, they will have enough time to find missing items, update shortage annexes, and print the current Technical Manuals. This will save you many hours of time during your inventory.

Personally, I conducted my incoming change-of-command inventory in five business days. We had property in multiple locations, too. I simply drafted up a game-plan and stuck with it. We did work some long hours, but we got the job done.

In closing, you might have heard horror stories from former Company Commanders who simply "signed for their property book" without ever conducting a proper inventory.

Unfortunately, when these commanders finished their command time and turned over the property to the new commander, they had missing equipment and ended up paying hundreds, even thousands of dollars to the government.

My advice to you is this: DON'T DO THAT. Be prepared. Remember, if you start your command time with an accurate and updated inventory, it's much easier to manage your property throughout your time in command.

On the other hand, if you start with discrepancies, it will cost you when you conduct your outgoing change of command inventory.

Be proactive. Be thorough when you conduct your initial inventory. While you are in command; conduct all inventories according to schedule and to standard. Be involved.

FINAL TIP:

It is in your best interest to sit down with the Supply Sergeant and Property Book Officer a few months before you take command.

Have them give you a class on inventories, share recommended resources and give you tips for success. It will be time well spent.

Chapter 5

Conducting Your Left-Seat-Right-Seat Ride

You've finished the change-of-command inventory and are about to take command.

Congratulations. One of the wisest things you can do now is conduct a "left-seat-right-seat-ride" with the outgoing commander.

In case you're not familiar with this term, it is simply another term for "job shadowing." A left-seat-right-seat-ride is when the incoming person and outgoing person work together.

The outgoing person teaches the incoming person the ropes. They can answer questions, review Standing Operating Procedures, discuss unit strengths and weaknesses, etc.

One of the smartest things you can do as the incoming commander is make a list of questions for the outgoing commander, BEFORE you conduct your left-seat-right-seat ride.

Take out a notepad and spend a couple of hours brainstorming potential questions. Ask former Company Commanders (that you know) which questions you should ask.

Some example questions may include:

- Knowing what you know right now, what would you have done differently during your time in command?
- What is your biggest regret while in command?

- What is your biggest accomplishment in command and why?
- If you could only give me one piece of advice, what would it be?
- What are the strengths of the unit?
- What are the weaknesses of the unit?
- What were your biggest challenges?
- What do you do to manage your time wisely?
- What should I do to make sure I am prepared for the job?
- Is the unit prepared to accomplish its wartime mission?
- What could I do to make the biggest, immediate impact?
- What is your daily routine?
- What tips do you have for working with higher headquarters?
- What am I not asking you that I should be asking you?

These are just a few questions you could ask.

In my opinion, **outgoing commanders are one of the greatest resources in the military**.

Unfortunately, many of them leave command without ever getting the opportunity to share that knowledge with their replacements. Don't let that happen to you.

Your biggest issue is TIME. You will have very limited time to meet with the outgoing commander.

Chances are, you both have civilian jobs and commitments, and will not be able to spend much time "job shadowing," except during your first drill weekend.

If that's the case, come up with a plan to talk on the phone, through email or through Instant Messaging.

Find a way to soak in their knowledge. Don't let their two-years of command experience simply walk away.

Be proactive. Chances are they're more than willing to share their insights and experience with you, if you ask. If they're not willing to do that, you have other alternatives.

You can talk with the First Sergeant and Company XO. You can also talk with other commanders in the battalion and former Company Commanders that you know. Most officers will gladly help out another officer.

One point to remember is that you don't have to do everything they recommend. You have your own personality, agenda and leadership style. But, at least get their insights and evaluate it at face value. It will make life a lot easier for you.

Chapter 6

Change-of-Command Ceremony

Once you sign for the property book, your battalion S1 will cut assumption of command orders. That will be the effective date you are the commander.

By now, you should have already conducted your inventory and your left-seat-right-seat ride.

In my opinion, <u>you MUST have a change-of-command ceremony</u>. It doesn't matter if there are 20 soldiers available or 200. It is a must. It establishes your credibility and authority, right from day one.

At a minimum you should have a formation of troops, your Battalion Commander, CSM, and your First Sergeant present.

Here are some things/questions to consider.

1. Set a date/time that works best for the key leaders (preferably during drill weekend)

2. Get specific guidance from the Battalion Commander how they want the ceremony to work

3. Get input from the CSM, 1SG and NCOs

4. The outgoing/incoming commander should sit down and determine any special requirements they want to take place

5. If food/refreshments need to be purchased, figure out who will pay for it (the incoming commander should pick up the tab for this)

6. As the incoming commander, ask the AGR Staff and outgoing commander if they want help planning the ceremony

7. Read the pertinent regulations to determine protocol

8. Ensure the outgoing commander will get some type of gift, and their spouse will also get something special, like flowers

9. Talk with at least three former Company Commanders to see what they recommend

10. Keep the ceremony simple, short and sweet (nothing extravagant)

In addition, the change-of-command ceremony isn't really about you (the incoming commander). It's about the outgoing Company Commander.

You owe it to them, whether they were squared away or not, to have a change of command ceremony. Pay them your respects, present them an award and send them on their way.

In most cases, the AGR Staff and command team will plan the change-of-command ceremony. They might ask you for your input, but don't be shocked if they don't. Just make sure you show up on time and complete the change of command ceremony.

Also, when you are giving your speech, remember the ceremony is not about you, it's about the outgoing commander.

Keep your speech short and to the point, preferably two minutes or less. You can give your big speech after you successfully finish your command time.

Once the ceremony is over, enjoy your moment or two of glory and get ready to work. The honey moon period will be over soon and your boss, the Battalion Commander, will expect you to either know what you're doing or act like you know what you're doing.

Part Two
Your First Year in Command

Chapter 7

Your First IDT Weekend

You're the new Company Commander! Congratulations.

You're driving to drill weekend for your first drill weekend as the new boss. You're anxious, excited and maybe even a little bit nervous. I know I was. You want to hit the ground running. You know what your objectives are for the weekend. You have a game-plan.

I hope this describes you. If it doesn't, you might need to adjust fire a bit. In my opinion, <u>your first drill weekend is critical for your long-term success</u>. You have a lot to accomplish, including some must-do things.

<u>During your first IDT weekend, you should:</u>

- Meet with your entire unit and share your command philosophy, vision and leadership style

- Conduct a formal Command Climate Survey

- Conduct a formal initial counseling, in writing, with your 1SG, XO and Platoon Leaders

- Visit each section/platoon area

- Complete Planned Training

- Conduct the After Action Review

Let's get into a little more detail.

At the first formation, you should introduce yourself to the entire unit. You should explain your leadership style, personality style, command philosophy, and vision for the organization.

You should clearly explain what is expected of each soldier (e.g. arrive at training on time, in the right uniform, ready to work, etc.).

If you've already published your policy letters, give each soldier a copy. You should also explain what will happen if soldiers fail to meet your expectations. Explain what will and will not be tolerated.

The best thing to do is to bring your soliders into a classroom or in the common area at the armory and give your 20-minute speech.

If possible, have your Battalion Commander or Battalion XO attend the meeting with you, so they can introduce you formally to your company, before you get up and speak. If they aren't available, have your First Sergeant read your bio to everyone.

Once you've shared this information with your soldiers, you should pull aside your direct reports, such as the First Sergeant, Company XO and Platoon Leaders and conduct their initial counseling with them.

You can verbally conduct each counseling session, informing them of their performance objectives, your standards, expectations, etc.

After drill weekend, and before the next drill weekend, you can type up and prepare each counseling statement "formally" with the proper forms and then have your direct reports review and sign the documents. You owe it to your direct reports to clearly inform them of what you expect of them.

<u>Make sure you put it in writing</u>. If it's not in writing, it didn't happen.

Next, you should have someone from outside your company conduct a Command Climate Survey to assess the "atmosphere" and "morale" within your unit. The information you collect will help you identify a plan of action and will help you set specific goals to meet, and shortcomings to overcome.

If that isn't possible, you can hand out a survey of your own for everyone to fill out. You could simply ask these three questions:

1 What is the one thing you like most about the unit?

2 What is the one thing you like least about the unit?

3 What is the one thing the Company Commander could do to improve the unit?

Even though my example survey isn't as formal as the Command Climate Survey, it's still helpful. And it's definitely better than doing nothing at all.

Regardless of whether you do a Command Climate Survey or your own survey, make sure you publish the results on a Memorandum for Record and give every soldier in your unit a copy. As the months go by, keep everyone updated on the progress and what your plan of action is.

Next, you should spend a couple of hours walking through the armory and visit each platoon or section area. Begin your initial assessment by asking questions, talking with soldiers and conducting formal or informal inspections on equipment, reports, and training. By doing so, you can begin relationship building and assess each section's readiness.

Finally, ensure all training is completed on time and to standard.

Your First Sergeant and Company XO should be the tip-of-the-spear during training, especially during your first drill weekend. Spend some time with them and assess their performance. Finally, at the end of training conduct a unit AAR.

If you do these things during your first drill weekend as the new Company Commander, you will be way above your peers. Your soldiers will know you are serious about what you do.

Remember, it's easier to start "hard core" and soften up, compared to starting soft and then trying to become hard-core later on. **You never get a second chance to make a first impression.**

Chapter 8

Your First 90 Days

Your first 90-days in Company Command can make you or break you. They are critical to establishing your credibility, effectiveness and reputation. Like everything you do, you must have a game-plan.

In the previous chapter, we discussed your first drill weekend, which in essence, is your first 30-days in command. In addition to those tasks, you have other tasks you should accomplish in your first 90-days.

My objectives for my first 90-days in Company Command were:

Month 1

- Conduct Unit Command Climate Survey (has to be done by day 90)
- Conduct Initial Counseling with your Rater, the Battalion Commander
- Conduct Initial Counseling with all Direct Reports
- Make Initial Assessments of Each Platoon
- Conduct Unit AAR
- Conduct Change of Command Ceremony (if not already completed)

Month 2

- Review Standing Operating Procedures & Tactical SOP
- Review Mission Essential Task List (METL) and submit proposed METL to Battalion Commander
- Conduct formal Platoon Inspections on Soldiers and Equipment
- Finish Initial Counseling with Direct Reports (have them sign their counseling statements)
- Review Key Metrics of Unit (Weapons Qual, APFT, MOSQ, etc.)
- Publish Your Command Philosophy (if you haven't already done so)

Month 3

- Conduct Officer Professional Development with officers
- Review Family Care Plans and Family Readiness Group
- Conduct Unit Level APFT to Assess Physical Fitness
- Review Unit Supply, Admin and Maintenance Areas (with Company XO)

Once again, these were my objectives. You don't have to have the same exact objectives that I did. However, you need some type of game-plan.

If you can't figure out what to do, just do what I recommended above.

Show your soldiers that you are the leader. Show them you have a game-plan. This will help you establish your credibility as a leader.

Chapter 9

Working with Your AGR Staff & Command Team

This might just be one of the most important chapters in this book.

I learned a long time ago that **no one is successful all by themselves.** *Successful leaders are either promoted or demoted, based upon the production of their team. Build a good team and you will succeed. Build a losing team and you will lose.*

Successful Company Commanders have great organizations. They create winning organizations.

Everything starts at the top and works its way down. The speed of the leader is the speed of the team. Please remember that.

A good commander can turn the Bad News Bears into the Chicago Bears® and a bad commander can turn the Chicago Bears® into the Bad News Bears.

Your job as the Company Commander is to work very closely with your command team, to empower them, and to make sure they have the motivation, training and resources they need to succeed.

You give them the guidance, the resources, and training, and then GET THE HELL OUT OF THEIR WAY so they can do their job. Trust me, they WANT the unit to succeed.

To succeed as a Company Commander, <u>you need to be</u> <u>of-the-spear</u>, but you also must rely on your First Sergeant, XO, Platoon Leaders and AGR Staff.

<u>Success is a team sport</u>. You cannot succeed by yourself. If you can work together, toward ONE common vision, amazing things can happen in the unit.

On other hand, if each person in the command team has their own agenda, chaos will soon follow. It is the Company Commander's responsibility to make sure the command team relationships are smooth and functional.

As an M-Day Company Commander in the USAR or ARNG, you have a much different situation than your active duty counterpart. You are not there full-time, day in and day out. Neither are your First Sergeant, XO or Platoon Leaders.

<u>That's why your full-time AGR staff will be the back-bone of your unit</u>. Let me say that again. **Your full-time AGR staff will be the back-bone of your unit.**

Don't get me wrong, the Company Commander, First Sergeant, XO and Platoon Leaders all have an important role, but in the National Guard and Army Reserve, the full-time AGR staff is the pulse of the organization. Your full-time staff handles the day-to-day activities (and issues) of your organization.

They receive calls from YOUR soldiers when there is a problem. They handle suspenses with your higher headquarters. They make decisions in your absence. <u>They can make you or break you</u>. Trust me on that one.

It is vitally important to develop a good working relationship with your AGR staff and command team. It is important to sit

n and clearly articulate what you expect of
ne lanes, establish standards, let them know
ct of them and let them know what they should
It's important to determine who is responsible for what, right from day one.

Each person should have **specific** objectives and responsibilities. When everyone knows what their "lane" is, there is no confusion. To clarify, these expectations MUST be in writing, via counseling.

I always told my support staff, "I don't want to do your job and I don't expect you to do my job."

Let's take a few minutes and discuss what each member of your command team should be responsible for. This might vary slightly based upon what type of unit you are in, but it's a good starting point.

Company Commander

I figured I would include a short description about what the Company Commander is supposed to do.

Your major responsibility is strategic planning. You set the vision for the organization and plan all upcoming training. This includes writing OPORDs, establishing policy, preparing training schedules, completing Risk Assessments and more.

Your second responsibility is collective training. Your job is to train and evaluate your squads, platoons and company on their collective tasks.

Finally, your third major focus is <u>leader development</u>. It's your job to make sure your officers and NCOs receive the development they need and deserve. This is done through military education, OPD/NCODP, and counseling.

Of course, you have many other responsibilities as well, but these are the big three as I see it.

Company XO

The Company XO is typically responsible for the supply, administration and maintenance within the unit.

Think of your XO as "current operations." If it's something that needs to be handled immediately, the XO is on it.

They work closely with the AGR Staff in a management capacity. They should know the status of all supply, administration and maintenance issues within the unit at all times. It's their job to stay on top of these things and keep you briefed.

It's their job to work closely with the AGR staff and make sure they have the training, resources and time to do their job.

If you remember nothing else, just remember <u>SUPPLY</u>, <u>ADMIN</u> and <u>MAINTENANCE</u> are the XO's biggest three responsibilities.

First Sergeant

The First Sergeant handles all soldier issues to include solider development, discipline, and individual training. This includes health, welfare and morale.

Individual training, such as PT, weapons training, MOS training and Warrior Task Training are the First Sergeant's primary focus. They also have a big role in soldier development, such as Sergeant's Time, NCODP, NCOERs, counseling and schools.

If you remember nothing else, remember SOLIDER DEVELOPMENT, DISCIPLINE, and INDIVIDUAL TRAINING.

Platoon Leaders

The Platoon Leaders are commanders of their platoons. Like you, their primary job includes strategic planning, collective training and leader development. They are the big picture thinkers who are focused on "future training." They plan, while the NCOs coordinate and resource. Their jobs are very similar to yours, just on a smaller scale.

If you remember nothing else, just remember that Platoon Leaders focus on STRATEGIC PLANNING, COLLECTIVE TRAINING and LEADER DEVELOPMENT.

Supply Sergeant

Your Supply Sergeant manages the unit property. They have custodial responsibility for the property.

They order clothing and equipment (OCIE and TA-50) for soldiers, oversee inventories, turn-in excess items, manage hand receipts, issue weapons (typically), order food for drill weekend, and work directly with the Battalion S4.

Basically, they make sure that your unit has the equipment and supplies it needs to have a successful drill weekend.

Training NCO

The Training NCO inputs information into the Army Training Requirements and Resources System (ATTRS). They schedule soldiers for MOS, NCOES, OES and professional development schools.

They resource training areas, equipment, personnel and resources for upcoming training events. This includes individual training and collective training.

Admin NCO

The Unit Administrative NCO manages the day-to-day correspondence within the unit. They update soldier records, SOPs, process personnel transactions, etc. This includes OERs, NCOERs, awards, SIDPERS and IPERMS issues, etc. Not all company level units have an Admin NCO, but some do.

Readiness NCO

The Readiness NCO is and should be the tip-of-the-spear for the AGR Staff. They should be a GO-GETTER.

The Readiness NCO manages the AGR Staff and typically processes pay, resolves soldier issues, submits reports, meets suspenses, oversees the AGR Staff, and makes decisions in the commander's absence.

This one person alone will have the biggest impact on your results as a Company Commander.

TIPS FOR SUCCESS

What I would like to do now is share some success tips that can really help you establish solid relationships with your command team.

Everything starts with <u>MUTUAL RESPECT</u> and <u>TRUST</u>. You must be able to trust each other. You must be able to communicate freely with each other (up and down communication).

When there is an issue, your command team must be able to approach you without worry of being crucified or chewed out. After all, <u>they are your trusted advisors</u>.

You must rely on each other. Do what you say. Say what you do. Be an impeccable example. Show them, by your actions, that you care about them as people, not just as soldiers.

Show them you are serious about what you do. <u>Show them that the UNIT and SOLDIERS are your # 1 priority, not yourself.</u> **Invest your time, money and energy into developing your command team.**

Make sure they get the schools, counseling and professional development they need to succeed. Build strong relationships with them. Take them out to lunch once in a while. Always have their back (as long as it's legal, moral and ethical).

Let them know that if they mess up, you will still support them. Let them know it's okay to make mistakes. Just make sure they learn from each mistake and don't make the same mistake twice. Let them know that you don't expect them to do your job, and you don't expect to do their job either.

They understand you are an M-Day Soldier. They know you have additional responsibilities outside of the military. However, they still expect you to be the Company Commander and ultimate decision maker.

- You plan for the missions
- You write the OPORDs and prepare training schedules
- You do the risk assessments
- You do the training calendar
- You run the meetings
- You make the tough decisions
- *You accept responsibility when things go wrong and give credit when things go right*

The buck stops with you. After all, it's your company! You are the Company Commander. **The quickest way to earn their respect is to be actively involved**.

Call the unit once a day for a few minutes and check in with them. See what you can do to make their life easier. See what you can do to help.

Share any valuable information you might have with them. Keep them informed. Have them do the same thing with you. Empower your command team. Let them know you BELIEVE in them.

Prepare OPORDs on time and disseminate the information quickly so they can resource it.

Have a weekly "follow up" call on SKYPE or conference line with your AGR staff and command team to find out what is going on, what they need from you, and find out what you can do to help.

<u>Show them that you care</u>. Show them that you are willing to do your job. Show them that you are the leader you are supposed to be.

So many ARNG and USAR Company Commanders sit back and let the AGR staff do everything. I think that is a big mistake. After all, the quickest way to lose their respect is to do nothing.

If you act like you're one of the troops, and just show up for training, you will never earn their respect.

<u>You cannot delegate your responsibility</u>. Be the tip-of-the-spear and they will want to follow you!

One last piece of advice here: be a servant leader. One of the best things you can do is <u>work for your AGR staff and command team</u>, rather than just think that they work for you.

What I mean by that is to support them, have their back, and make sure they get the resources they need to succeed in their jobs. Be involved and do what you can to help out.

Chapter 10

Balancing Command, Family Time & Life

I'm really not qualified to write this chapter, but I will give it my best shot. *Company Command is very time consuming, even as an M-Day Soldier.* There is nothing part-time about it.

One of my former mentors once told me that <u>command will take as much time from you as you are willing to give it</u>. If you can invest 10-hours per week, it will take it. If you give it 30-hours a week, it will take that too.

If you're going to accept the position as Company Commander, you need to make some personal sacrifices. You'll probably work at least 15-20 hours unpaid each week, outside of drill weekend.

You will need to give up some of your civic activities or hobbies for a couple of years, until your command time is finished. <u>While you're in command, you will live your life out-of-balance</u>.

Even if you're efficient and effective at what you do, you will invest a good deal of your free time to get your job done. Most of your work will be done on your own time, outside of drill weekend.

In most cases, you will not be financially compensated for your time. You need to know that upfront.

If you're single and do not have kids, you might have a slight advantage over someone who is married with kids. If you have a spouse and kids, you just need to be more aware of how much time you spend doing your job.

Obviously, you don't want to get "the speech" from your spouse or your employer. You need to fulfill your role as a husband or wife, and fulfill your day job obligations, so you don't get fired.

That being said, I would recommend to everyone before they take command to have a heart-to-heart conversation with their spouse, outlining the duties and responsibilities they will be expected to perform.

Let them know about your monthly battalion and company training meetings. Talk to them about unplanned armory visits and occasional "fires" you will have to put out. That way there are no surprises once you take command.

During my time in command, I probably averaged 20-hours per week unpaid, which included, on average, one visit per week to the armory (1-hour drive each way).

At times, it did put a strain on my business and on my marriage. My secret to success was to communicate with my wife about what I had to do. I also gave up hobbies and other things while in command.

If I would have had a traditional job, (I own my own business and work from home) I wouldn't have been able to commit as much time to my command as I did.

I've found that Company Commanders who are technicians or AGR have a HUGE advantage over other commanders, because they can do their command work at their AGR or technician job. However, most M-Day commanders do not have that luxury.

As you can probably tell, Company Command isn't for everyone. You owe it to your troops to give them your best. If you're not willing to live 18-24 months out-of-balance, you should pass on becoming a Company Commander.

Knowing this information up front is half the battle.

Your time in command will go by quickly. Hopefully, you will be able to look back with pride. Hopefully, you can overlook the sacrifices and focus on what you accomplished.

Before, I close out this chapter, I can offer you a few tips on how to keep things in balance.

1 Create a Routine & Set Work Hours

One of the best things you can do is come up with some type of weckly routine. Set "work hours" for certain times on certain days of the week.

For instance, maybe you do your Company Commander duties every Tuesday and Thursday night from 7 to 9 p.m. at home. Find a way to block off at least 8-10 hours per week to do your military work at home.

2 Empower Your Subordinates

Like it or not, you are going to have to rely on your AGR staff a lot. They understand that.

I suggest you have a heart-to-heart conversation with them when you first take command and make sure that everyone has clear expectations about who will do what.

In addition, I HIGHLY suggest you empower your XO, First Sergeant and Platoon Leaders. This is a team sport. You are not the only one who will have to sacrifice some free time. It comes with being a leader.

Besides, your command team is more capable than you realize. Give them some tough assignments to find out what they are good at and what their strengths are.

They will appreciate the opportunity to showcase their talents, and more than likely, they will rise to the occasion.

3 Set Priorities

<u>You can't do it all</u>. Most of the time, you will feel like you are putting twenty pounds of stuff into a five-pound bag. Not everything will get done.

You need to establish priorities and determine what is really important to you. <u>Keep the main thing the main thing</u>. Just because something is urgent doesn't mean that it's important and it doesn't mean that you have to do it yourself.

Remember that mission planning, collective training, and leader development are your big three priorities. 80% of your time should be spent on those things.

4 Schedule Family & Personal Time

This is one thing I wish I would have done while I was in command. I suggest you get a day planner and schedule in family time each week. Make sure you schedule in a date night with your spouse, time with your kids, time for the gym, and time for some personal activities. If you "schedule it" it will happen. If you don't schedule it, it won't happen.

FINAL TIP

When it comes to managing your time, you can manage it or it will manage you. The best thing I can suggest is to get a day planner and schedule in your work, Army, family and personal commitments. Track them out as far as you can. Manage your time by the hour if necessary. Get organized and develop a time management system that works for you.

Otherwise, you will burn the candle at both ends.

Chapter 11

Your Typical Monthly Schedule

Once you've been in Company Command for a few months, you will establish a battle rhythm.

Each battalion operates differently. You will have to come up with your own schedule, based upon how your battalion, or higher headquarters, does things.

Here's how our battalion did things:

- Scheduled Training Event (IDT weekend or Annual Training)
- 7-10 Days Later: Battalion Training Meeting
- 7-10 Days Later: Company Training Meeting
- 7-10 Days Later: Drill Weekend
- Repeat the following month

Typically, 7-10 days after drill weekend, your unit will have a Battalion Training Meeting to review future training (up to 120-days out) and to review recent training events. These meetings are usually held on a weeknight and are conducted in person or via tele-conference.

Once you've finished the battalion's training meeting, you will sift and sort through the information and prepare a Company OPORD detailing your unit requirements.

At your Company Training Meeting (7 to 10-days after the battalion's meeting), you will share this information with your AGR Staff, Company XO, 1SG, Platoon Leaders and Platoon Sergeants.

Your full-timers, Platoon Leaders and PSGs will further plan and resource the requirements. They will then have a Platoon Training Meeting.

About 7-10 days later, you will have your next drill weekend. You will execute the training, assess the training, and conduct an AAR. Once the training weekend is over, the cycle starts all over again.

In addition to the items we just discussed, you will also have additional unplanned and unscheduled requirements outside of your scheduled training.

This includes inspections, Yearly Training Calendar planning, ceremonies, TAG and ATAG briefings, NGAUS Conferences, and much more. Sometimes these events are planned well ahead of time. Other times, they are very short notice. Regardless, you are expected to attend the training event.

Be a good leader and attend these events. It comes with the job. Ensure that you carry your calendar with you at all times. When you get information, update your calendar and share the information with your subordinates (if it pertains to them).

What you really need to do is come up with a routine or battle rhythm that you can follow. This will make life a lot easier for you and your command team. We are all creatures of habit and most people like routines.

I suggest you sit down with your AGR staff and command team when you first take command and come up with some type of battle rhythm. It might change a little bit in the months to come, as you get better at your job and look for things you can improve upon.

The bottom line is that you need a battle rhythm and weekly schedule, so you know what to expect.

Part Three
The Big Things

Chapter 12

Training Management

One of your major responsibilities as the Company Commander is Training Management.

Your ultimate job is to ensure your unit is trained and prepared to accomplish its wartime mission. That is your most important task. Everything else is secondary.

You want your unit to have the SKILL (training) and WILL (motivation).

Since the 9/11 attacks, the Army Reserve and National Guard have been used more and more as an operational force, rather than a reserve force.

That means that the likelihood of your unit deploying overseas is quite high. In fact, most Army Reserve and National Guard units have already deployed at least once. Some units have deployed two, even three or more times.

What can you do to train your unit effectively? That appears to be the million-dollar question.

Your major role as the Company Commander is to PLAN tough, safe and realistic training.

All of your training needs to be battle-focused. Train like you fight. Get the hell out of the armory, and go to the field (or a training site) and conduct some battle-focused training.

Your soldiers must be proficient as soldiers (shoot, move and communicate), with their MOS, and proficient in your unit's collective training.

Next, you must ensure your training is properly resourced. Once that's completed you need to conduct training, to standard. Finally, you must evaluate and assess training.

Let's cover these in a little more detail.

PLANNING TRAINING:

As the Company Commander, you establish your training objectives with the Battalion Commander. You submit a proposed Yearly Training Calendar (YTC) for approval. You submit your Company METL for approval. And you create training schedules.

In addition, you will write monthly OPORDs detailing each training event.

To set yourself up for success, you should be very familiar with the Battalion YTC. You must create training schedules for your company; detailing the task, purpose, location, equipment requirements, etc.

You should have your OPORDs written at least 30-days ahead of time, so you can utilize the 1/3 – 2/3 rule.

If that's not possible, at least publish a Warning Order to give your subordinate leaders whatever information you do have, so they can do their own planning.

The Army utilizes FM 7-0 as its Training Bible (the number of the actual FM might change through the years).

Get a copy. You can download it off the Internet. Start familiarizing yourself with it now. Read it and take notes. Study it.

Remember, <u>your job as the Company Commander is to focus on collective training</u>.

Typically, your First Sergeant's job is to focus on individual training. The two go hand-in-hand.

If you plan properly, your unit will have time to conduct both individual and collective training during every drill weekend.

While I was in Company Command, I tried to spend about 70% of my working time <u>outside</u> of drill weekend doing mission PLANNING.

I wrote OPORDs, did Risk Assessments, drafted training schedules, conducted mission analysis and more.

This type of work was generally done in my personal time, between drill weekends. It was a very time-consuming task. However, it enabled my unit to always be adequately prepared for each training event.

RESOURCING TRAINING:

I utilized my full-time AGR staff to resource all training requirements. After all, most companies have a full-time Training NCO and Readiness NCO.

If you draft a well thought out OPORD, your full-time Training NCO should easily be able to resource what is needed, such as training areas, ammunition, equipment and logistics.

If you don't have a full-time Training NCO, your Readiness NCO will have to pick up the slack.

The secret to success is to plan ahead of time and IDENTIFY all required resources, so they know what the unit needs.

A key point to remember is that many installations require you to lock-in resources 90 to 120-days out, sometimes even longer.

Be proactive. Look at your YTC each month. Make sure you have requested the required resources for 90 to 180-days out. Sit down with your AGR Staff and see what progress they have made. Double check their work. Ask them if they need help with anything.

Be involved in the resourcing and coordinating process. You won't have a lot to do in this process, but do what you can to help out your AGR staff.

One thing that really helped me out in this area was building a relationship with the Battalion S3 SGM and Operations Officer. Most of your requests will initially be sent through the S3 Shop anyway.

Get in their hip pocket. Ask either of them questions about training management. They will gladly help you.

At least one of them is part of the AGR force and will readily be available to help. Besides, they like it when the Company Commanders are actively involved and doing their job like they are supposed to.

CONDUCTING TRAINING:

Unlike our Active Duty counterparts, we only have two to three days each month to conduct training. That's why the preparation phase is so important. If you plan properly, your training should go smoothly.

The secret to conducting realistic training is to be prepared, start on time, and to brief your soldiers on the task, purpose and standards.

Give them a safety brief. Ensure your resources are on hand and operational. Then, let your NCOs take over and execute the training.

Your job is to supervise and assess. A lot of commanders make the mistake of being too involved in this stage of the training process. They're so gung-ho and eager that they forget what their real role is.

Yes, you should be on site. Yes, you should be involved (to some degree). But let your NCOs shine. Let them do their job. Let your Platoon Leaders and XO do their job. Be present, but stay out of their way!

EVALUATE & ASSESS TRAINING:

Once your unit's scheduled training is finished, conduct an After-Action-Review, also known as an AAR.

As the Company Commander, you should lead the AAR. Start with the training objective. Then talk about what was supposed to happen. Then review what actually happened.

Ask your soldiers what they thought went well and what went wrong. Ask questions like "what could we have been done better?" Seek input from all ranks.

Get everyone to participate and provide feedback. Once the training is complete, your job is to update your Mission Essential Task Listing (METL) assessment. In addition, you should publish the results of your AAR and give everyone in your unit a copy (and post one to the unit bulletin board).

SUMMARY:

National Guard and Army Reserve units must be prepared to deploy at moment's notice, in order to help fight and win our nation's wars. Ultimately, that responsibility lies on each Company Commander.

You must take "training" very seriously. You must properly plan, resource, conduct and evaluate every training exercise. You must train as you fight and train safely. Your soldiers lives depend upon it.

Chapter 13

Unit Administration

Paperwork! Reports! As much as I hate paperwork, it is important. Some of it.

Your job as the commander is to ensure the required paperwork is done correctly and on time. Your job is not to create unneeded, additional paperwork, or do everything yourself.

Some of the important paperwork includes:

- Personnel Action on DA 4187
- Awards
- Training Requests
- OERs and NCOERs
- STAP/Enlisted/Officer Promotions
- Extensions and Reenlistments
- DA 1379 for Drill Pay
- OPORDs and Risk Assessments

That's just a small example of paperwork you'll find at the small unit level.

You will quickly learn that just about every piece of paper that leaves your unit will require your signature on it. You should consider doing a "signature delegation" to your Readiness NCO (if you trust them).

This will give them authority to sign certain types of documents for you. If that's not possible, they can scan and email you the documents to sign.

Your Administration NCO should be on top of things. Ensure that they use a tracking number (TL) when they send documents outside of your unit. Ensure everything is tracked, so when your unit is accused of not submitting paperwork on time, you will have proof to prove otherwise.

One of the most important things for you to do is to always be PROMPT. Don't wait a couple of weeks to sign a document. Be proactive.

<u>That piece of paper is important to someone, even if it's not all that important to you.</u> It affects someone in your unit.

There are few things worse than not being able to accomplish something, simply because someone didn't sign the document.

I have a few good tips that worked for me when it comes to paperwork.

First of all, empower your XO to step up to the plate. Put them in charge of evaluation reports, awards and risk assessments.

Let them be the "lead" in ALL administration issues. Have them brief you each week on the status of these documents. By all means, be involved yourself, but empower them to do this. It's a big part of their job.

Next, I suggest you create some type of tracking document for your important paperwork. Have an Excel® spreadsheet, a dry erase board, or some type of mechanism where you can track the current status of your important paperwork. Have your AGR staff update it frequently and keep you and the XO informed.

My final tip is to keep a close eye on the paperwork, and make sure it gets done, but don't let it control you.

Yes, paperwork is important. But as the Company Commander, <u>your real job is PEOPLE and TRAINING</u>. *Don't confuse the forest for the trees.*

The bottom line is that there is a lot of paperwork generated at the unit level. Your ultimate job is to make sure the paperwork is done and processed on time and to standard, but not to do everything yourself.

Empower your Company XO and AGR staff to keep a finger on the pulse and everything will work out fine.

Chapter 14

Unit Supply

Let me begin by telling you that this chapter does not discuss EVERYTHING you need to know about unit supply. My goal is to simply give you an overview of the basic requirements.

One of the quickest ways to get relieved of your duties (other than pay or EO issues) is to not properly maintain accountability and serviceability of your unit's equipment.

Each unit has a property book. Your property book shows what equipment is authorized, in what quantity and shows what equipment is actually on hand.

You should always have a copy of the "updated and current" property book with you in your leader's book. Any time there is a change, from turning-in excess equipment or receiving new equipment, have your Supply Sergeant print you an updated copy.

At each drill weekend or at the unit training meeting, have the Supply Sergeant brief the status of supply (make sure the Company XO is working closely with the Supply Sergeant on this).

Have them discuss lateral transfers, equipment fielding, OCIE issues, the status of funds to order new equipment, hand-receipt issues, etc.

Don't neglect this area. I know you are busy and have a lot on your plate. It's even tempting to hand everything over to your Company XO.

While you should have the Company XO be the tip-of-the-spear with supply, you are still the one who is signed for everything. And if something goes wrong in supply, you will be the one that is held accountable. You are the primary hand receipt holder. Never forget that.

WHAT YOU NEED TO KNOW ABOUT SUPPLY:

The first thing to know about supply is that you have command responsibility for all supplies and equipment within your unit. When you first signed the hand receipt at your change-of-command inventory, you accepted that responsibility.

In addition to your command responsibility, your officers, NCOs and soldiers are also responsible for the safeguarding and maintaining of government equipment.

AR 735-5 outlines the five types of responsibility. In essence, they are:

1. **Command.** A commander is responsible for all property within their command.

2. **Supervisory.** A leader is responsible for property in the possession of the personnel they supervise.

3. **Direct.** The accountable officer is responsible for property not issued on a hand receipt, and the primary hand receipt holder is responsible for property accepted on hand receipt from the accountable officer.

4. **Custodial.** The supply sergeant, supply custodian, supply clerk, or warehouse person is responsible for property in storage awaiting issue or turn-in.

5. **Personal.** Each person is responsible for exercising reasonable and prudent actions to properly use, care for, safeguard, and dispose of all government property issued for, acquired for, or converted to his exclusive use, with or without receipt.

To set yourself up for success, you and your Supply Sergeant MUST sub-hand receipt your equipment to each Platoon Leader or Platoon Sergeant.

The Platoon Leader and Platoon Sergeant MUST further sub-hand receipt the equipment to the end user. That is what's supposed to happen.

Don't be the Company Commander who hasn't sub-hand receipted anything to anyone.

Empower your subordinates by giving them responsibility. Counsel them in writing about your expectations of them to safeguard your equipment. And make sure their hand receipt is accurate, current and signed.

UNIT SUPPLY SOP:

If your unit doesn't have a Unit Supply SOP, get one quickly.

Have your Company XO and Supply Sergeant work together to prepare a first draft. There's no need to start from scratch. Ask other Supply Sergeants within your battalion for a copy of their SOP. If they don't have one, do a quick Internet search. There are plenty of examples online.

A Unit Supply Standing Operating Procedure (SOP) should be built around the provisions of AR 190–11, Physical Security of Arms, Ammunition and Explosives; AR 710–2; AR 735–5; Department of the Army (DA) Pamphlet 710–2–1, Using Unit Supply System (Manual Procedures); command policy letters; and local SOPs.

AR 710–2 governs the processes that should be used in daily supply activities, and DA Pamphlet 710–2–1 tells you how to conduct these processes by providing examples of applicable forms.

If you already have a Supply SOP, validate it. Check to see if any regulations have changed. Review it to see if it still makes sense.

Are you actually conducting supply operations in accordance with your SOP? If not, revise your SOP to how you currently conduct business.

Make sure you review the Supply SOP at least once a year and make any changes as needed.

INVENTORIES:

Your Property Book Officer will publish an inventory schedule for your unit. This includes your sensitive and cyclic inventory.

In my opinion, you should physically participate in all unit inventories. Even if you're not the one doing the inventory yourself, you should be involved, to spot check, and to ensure your subordinates are doing the inventory properly.

You shouldn't take things at face value, especially when it comes to equipment accountability. If your Supply Sergeant and NCOs who actually conduct the inventory know that you never spot-check their work, they are less likely to be detailed or thorough.

Remember, **it's your property**. You are responsible for it. Inspect and verify.

OTHER CONSIDERATIONS:

In addition to what we've already mentioned, your Supply Sergeant and Company XO will also handle the Command Supply Discipline Program, external inspections, lateral transfers, equipment fielding and they will be actively involved with ordering and storing MREs, food and rations.

Do yourself a favor and be involved. Develop a basic understanding of what your Supply Sergeant should be doing. Talk with your Supply Sergeant at least once a week and have them brief you.

Here are some good questions to ask them on a regular basis:

1. What is the status of pending lateral transfers?
2. What equipment do we need to turn in this month?
3. Are we expecting any new equipment fielding in the near future?
4. When were the shortage annexes last updated?
5. When is the next scheduled inventory?
6. Do we have any PBO or BN S4 visits or inspections in the near future?
7. Are there any open issues I need to know about?

8. What is the supply status for our upcoming drill weekend?

9. What supply related issues should I be concerned about?

10. What issues do you need my help with?

11. Are there any changes to the property book this month?

Also, have your BN S4 and Company XO conduct occasional spot checks to ensure your company complies with Army policies.

SUMMARY:

One of the quickest ways to get fired as a Company Commander is to improperly handle unit supply.

You will spend many hours "spot-checking," "verifying," and "overseeing" unit supply. It's quite easy to place "unit supply" on the back-burner.

With all of the additional requirements and with the limited training time, it's easy to forget about. Do yourself a favor and "don't forget about it."

If you have a Company XO, supply will be their "baby." Just spot-check to ensure your Company XO and Supply Sergeant are on top of things.

Chapter 15

Unit Maintenance

In the previous chapter, we discussed Unit Supply. In addition to properly "accounting for" your equipment, you must also maintain it.

Since 9/11 the National Guard and Army Reserve have transformed from a reserve force to an operational force. Therefore, your equipment must be ready to deploy at a moment's notice.

Traditionally, the National Guard and Army Reserve are known for having old, outdated equipment. New equipment fieldings are generally reserved for the Active Duty component.

Usually, the National Guard and Army Reserve get the Active Duty's old equipment after they've been given new equipment.

In addition to having older equipment, the National Guard conducts maintenance much differently than the Active Duty Army does. On Active Duty, most battalions have access to maintenance personnel 24/7.

If a piece of equipment is dead-lined, especially a Pacing item, the Unit Commander can keep the mechanics on-site until the equipment is repaired.

In the National Guard things don't work that way. Since the units only train two or three days per month, most units PMCS their equipment during drill weekend.

Based upon their MTOE, most units can only conduct operator level-maintenance. If the unit has mechanics assigned to it, they can conduct "field-level" maintenance. However, some companies don't have any maintenance personnel assigned to their units. Instead, they rely on the FMS shops or external units to repair their equipment.

Once the equipment is PMCS'd by the operator, and the faults have been identified, the equipment is turned-over to the Field Maintenance Shops (FMS). Typically, each FMS shop supports five to ten different units or armories. Sometimes your unit equipment will "sit" at the FMS shop for six months or longer.

As the Company Commander, **I believe it's completely unacceptable to have equipment dead-lined that long.** It's also frustrating to have to turn your equipment over to someone else to fix.

I've always believed that commanders need CONTROL over their maintenance personnel. That way they can have their equipment fixed immediately. After all, no one cares about YOUR equipment as much as you do!

The major challenge in the National Guard and Army Reserve is the force structure and funding. Not only do most units not have their own maintenance section, but in many cases, there is no money to order parts!

WHAT DOES ALL OF THIS MEAN?

When you conduct training, maintenance must be a top priority. You must ensure all equipment is accurately PMCS'd by your Soldiers using a technical manual.

The faults must be accurately recorded onto the proper form and updated into SAMS-E. You must also complete your scheduled services on time and to standard.

Your Property Book Unit Supply Enhanced (PBUSE) tracks your other equipment, such as gas masks, night-vision devices, etc.

In addition, your vehicles are normally tracked in SAMS-E. All equipment must get PMCS'd and receive its scheduled services, too. This area often gets neglected. Don't let these things slack.

You will have 100 different things going on during drill weekend. <u>You must make maintenance a top priority</u>. You must find a way to ensure ALL equipment is properly maintained.

If your unit does not have internal maintenance assets, coordinate through your Battalion S4 and ask for additional resources during drill weekend. If you don't maintain your equipment, your equipment will not be operational when you need it. And that will create major problems!

To close out this chapter, I want to share a few maintenance tips that worked well for me. These are five things that every Company Commander should do (as I see it) when it comes to maintenance.

1 026 Report

Have your Company XO and Motor Sergeant keep an updated copy of your unit's 026 report. The 026 report lists all of your dead-lined equipment.

Make sure that they can brief you on the status of each piece of dead-lined equipment. They should know how long the equipment has been dead-lined, what it has been dead-lined for, the status of the parts on order, the status of the job, and the expected date it will be fixed.

Your Company XO and Motor Sergeant should send you updates by email at least once a week. You should also talk about maintenance during your training meeting.

2 Schedule Time for PMCS during Drill Weekend

As the Company Commander you control the training schedule. Make sure that you set aside time to do PMCS during every drill weekend. Put it on the training schedule. During PMCS, make sure that you are in the motor-pool with your soldiers. PMCS a vehicle yourself.

Make sure that everyone is using a Technical Manual and doing it the right way. If your subordinate leaders and soldiers know it is important to you, it will also become important to them.

3 Get to Know the Full-Time Maintenance Personnel

One of the best things you can do is get to know the Shop Chief in charge of your maintenance, outside of drill weekend.

If you don't have a Field Maintenance Shop supporting you, get to know WHOEVER is in charge of helping you maintain your equipment. Take them out to lunch. Find out what their policies and procedures are. Find out how the relationship is supposed to work.

Do what you can to build a good relationship with these maintenance folks.

4 Educate Yourself About Maintenance

Even if you don't have much of a background in maintenance, take some time and educate yourself.

Read a few Field Manuals. Read the unit SOP. Talk with some maintenance folks and find out how things should work. Talk with the Battalion Maintenance Officer. Even better, find an old Warrant Officer or NCO with a solid maintenance background and pick their brain for an hour or two.

The more you know about maintenance, the better you will be at your job. No, you don't need to be an expert about everything, but you do need some basic knowledge so you are informed.

5 Create a Unit Maintenance SOP

Another helpful thing you can do is create a good Unit Maintenance SOP. Start out by reviewing the current SOP. If it makes sense, keep using it.

The first thing you should do is read it yourself and have a few of your key leaders review it. Make any necessary changes.

If you don't have an SOP in place, get a copy of a sister unit's SOP and use that as a base document. Once you have a final version in place, make sure you review it annually and make any changes as needed.

Final Thoughts

Doing these five things will have a big impact on your unit's maintenance program. The bottom line is that maintenance is vitally important to your overall success.

Chapter 16

Retention

From the day you first take command, you will receive countless "top-down" messages about the importance of retention. You'll get briefs, OPORDs, senior officer visits and many other things to "stress" the importance of retaining your soldiers.

Personally, I've always believed that if you create a "winning atmosphere" where soldiers feel like they belong to something greater than themselves, your retention will take care of itself.

<u>Soldiers want tough, challenging training</u>. They do not want to show up at the armory and just "sit around" the entire drill weekend.

They want to do something exciting and challenging, such as shoot their weapons, conduct a ruck-march, conduct a convoy, or go to the field.

If you PLAN good, tough training and execute that training to standard, you will not have a retention problem in your unit. If you don't have tough, realistic training, you will have retention problems.

Another effective way to be proactive with your retention program is to review your ETS roster once each month. Have your Readiness NCO print out a copy prior to your drill weekend. Draft up a list of all soldiers with an ETS date within in the next 12-months.

During drill weekend, talk with each soldier individually that is scheduled to ETS within the next 120-days.

Find out about their personal situation. Ask them questions. Find out if they are happy with their MOS. If not, ask them if they want to re-class. Also, find out if they are happy with the unit or if there are any schools they want to attend.

If you show a genuine interest in your soldiers' needs and help them find solutions to their problems, they will extend and stay in. At least, most of them will. Most soldiers that ETS can be salvaged beforehand.

If you find out what they want, and show them how to get it, they will gladly stay in and continue their military service.

Another thing to consider is that there's nothing wrong with a soldier who does his or her time honorably and then decides to leave the military.

Although you are normally encouraged to retain everyone (or try to) <u>I truly believe your job is to help your soldier decide what is best for them</u>. As a caring leader, that is the right strategy to follow.

Many soldiers and Army officers are "chastised" for wanting to leave the military. I think that's wrong. If someone decides to ETS or get out, make sure they leave on a positive note.

Thank them for their service. Tell them how much you appreciate everything they did for the unit. And make sure you let them know that the door is always open if they want to come back.

The last thing you want is soldiers leaving the Army with a negative taste in their mouth. If you treat people with respect, and show a genuine interest in supporting their goals they might still leave the military, but they will leave the military on a positive note and might consider rejoining in the future.

In addition, when they talk to their friends, they will probably say "good things" about your unit and the National Guard/Army Reserve.

<u>Remember, retention is your responsibility</u>. Whether you like it or not, YOU will be held accountable for the strength and retention in your unit. Do your job and be proactive in this area.

Furthermore, before you talk to your soldier about extending, do some research and find out if they are eligible for a bonus. Find out how much time the soldier already has invested in the military. Help them calculate what their retirement pension would be if they stayed in. Get creative.

Investing a little time with each soldier lets them know that you care about them as a person, not just as a person on the books.

On the other hand, I've found that some soldiers shouldn't be retained. **You should focus your efforts on retaining the "good" soldiers, not your problem soldiers.**

If someone does nothing but cause problems and doesn't contribute any value to the organization, do what you can (legally of course) to make sure they don't reenlist.

The last thing you want is dirt bag soldiers moving up through the ranks on your watch! Your job is to sift and sort through your good and bad soldiers and spend your time retaining quality soldiers.

Chapter 17

Physical Fitness

The National Guard and Army Reserve have a bad reputation for having soldiers that are fat and out-of-shape. Compared to our Active Duty counterparts, our units typically have more overweight and out-of-shape soldiers.

One of the major constraints within the National Guard and Army Reserve is trying to maintain soldiers' physical fitness outside of drill weekend.

As part-time soldiers, most of our soldiers maintain jobs in the corporate world and only conduct two to three days of Army training each month.

Unfortunately, a high percentage of soldiers do not maintain their physical fitness on their own. They do not exercise on a regular basis, get adequate sleep or eat properly. As a result, they fail their APFT and/or HT/WT.

Visit most units and you will discover that 20-30% of ALL assigned soldiers FAIL one or both of these two events. In addition, you will find many soldiers who haven't passed the APFT in YEARS. Personally, I think that's wrong.

I believe leaders have a responsibility to hold people accountable to the Army standards. Furthermore, I've found that many units do not have time allocated for PT. In my opinion, even if your unit did, it wouldn't make a huge difference in the soldiers' physical fitness.

Conducting PT during drill weekend (2-days a month), but doing nothing the other 28-days is of little value to the individual soldier.

On the other hand, if your unit does PT during drill weekend, your soldiers will know that it is a high priority for you. I think it's better to do company level PT every drill weekend, compared to not doing it.

Remember, as the Company Commander, you are responsible for the readiness of your unit. Physical Fitness has a direct impact on your unit's readiness. You should find creative ways to incorporate PT into your training calendar.

More importantly, are you going to lead from the front? The worst thing you can do is get fat and not be able to pass the APFT or HT/WT yourself. If you can't pass it, don't expect your soldiers to. Make sure you stay in shape. If you need help, hire a dietician and personal trainer. But don't let yourself go.

In addition, you should conduct company-wide APFTs. Let your soldiers see you taking the APFT with the company. You and your First Sergeant should be the first ones in line, where your soldiers can see you.

Whenever possible, always conduct company-level APFTs, so there are no accusations about whether or not someone actually took or passed the APFT.

Furthermore, you need to develop and publish a written PT policy. Your policy should discuss what will happen to PT or HT/WT failures. What will you do if someone fails? Give everyone a copy of your PT Policy and make sure they are briefed on it.

My standard from day one was to let my soldiers know what I expected of them concerning physical fitness.

My expectations were that they would pass Height /Weight and the APFT once a year. If they didn't, they would be FLAGGED until they did pass.

They would also be enrolled in FIT-P and have 90-days to pass a second APFT. Anyone failing a second APFT would receive something additional, such as a Bar to Reenlistment or separation paperwork.

Once they were FLAGGED, no favorable personnel action could happen. If they retook the APFT at a later date and passed, I would lift/remove the FLAG.

By doing this, my soldiers knew I was serious. Most of the soldiers who failed one APFT got themselves in shape and passed the next one.

Unfortunately, many Company Commanders do nothing when someone fails the APFT or HT/WT.

I've always believed the Company Commander should always enforce the standards equally to everyone within their organization. It's simply the right thing to do. And it is part of being a good leader.

You should decide from day one, what you will do if someone fails the APFT or HT/WT. Whatever you decide, make sure you are consistent with everyone in your organization.

If your policy is to FLAG APFT failures, make sure you FLAG the First Sergeant if he fails too, not just your lowest ranking Private. <u>Once you've identified your APFT failures, help them.</u>

When possible, utilize programs the National Guard and Army Reserve already have in place. For instance, the Maryland National Guard has what is known as FIT-P.

It's a three-month (1 drill weekend per month) course where soldiers learn about dieting and exercising. It's a great course that helps a lot of soldiers.

If you don't have that resource available in your state, you could request a "Master Fitness Trainer" visit your unit to provide training. You could also see if a local dietician or personal trainer would visit your unit during IDT weekend to educate your soldiers about diet and exercise.

Or, you can have a Remedial PT program at the beginning or end of every Saturday and Sunday during drill weekend. Anyone who failed either event would be required to participate.

The bottom line is to get creative and find ways to help your soldiers stay in shape. Do what you can to make sure your soldiers pass the APFT and whatever you do, hold people who don't meet the standards accountable. Make sure you FLAG your APFT failures and document it in counseling and on their evaluation reports.

Chapter 18

Family Readiness

Family Readiness is really important for the morale and well-being of both the soldier and their loved ones.

Your job as the Company Commander is to sustain family readiness. This consists of maintaining a Family Readiness Group and ensuring required soldiers have updated Family Care Plans.

A Family Readiness Group, in essence, is a support group for family members, friends and loved ones.

The FRG consists of the spouses and family members of your Soldiers. The FRG typically has an informal chain-of-command.

The purpose of the FRG is to share information and provide support. Soldiers, spouses, friends, family-members or parents can participate. During deployments, FRGs are vital.

Some of the things that FRGs do include:

- Have meetings to share information
- Conduct unit fund raisers
- Conduct Family Day
- Provide support to each other while soldiers are deployed
- Create and disseminate newsletters

If your unit doesn't already have an FRG in place, start one. Ask soldiers to talk to their spouses to see if they are interested in starting a group.

Schedule a date. Email all soldiers and family members with the WHO, WHAT, WHY, WHEN, and WHERE for the first meeting. When people arrive at the meeting, give a short presentation about the purpose of FRGs.

Ask for volunteers. Get started. It doesn't have to be perfect. Over a period of time, your group will evolve. If you keep it as a high priority, it will get done.

If you already have an FRG in place, you're lucky.

Your job is to support the FRG. Do they have the required resources? Talk with the FRG Coordinator on a regular basis. Seek their input. Find ways to help them.

Typically, I've found that most soldiers and units are hesitant to start a FRG during peace-time. However, once a unit has orders to deploy the interest escalates overnight.

Your job as the leader is to have once in place, so when your unit receives deployment orders, you can worry about deployment prep and training, while your FRG helps family members.

FAMILY CARE PLANS:

Single soldiers with dependents and dual military soldiers are required to have Family Care Plans.

As the Company Commander, your job is to identify soldiers who need a Family Care Plan, counsel them, validate their plan and review it on an annual basis. This is a really important task.

It may be one more thing on your plate, but it comes down to "taking care of soldiers." Do it. Plus, it's something you aren't allowed to delegate.

MONTHLY NEWSLETTER:

One thing that worked well in our unit was having a monthly email newsletter.

We discussed upcoming training, reviewed prior month's training, and shared unit and soldier accomplishments. We emailed this to all soldiers and any interested family members.

I found it to be an effective way to communicate with everyone in the company. I highly recommend you create a monthly email newsletter for your unit.

FACEBOOK PAGE:

Just about everyone is on Facebook. I suggest you create a fan page or secret group for your unit on Facebook. Have everyone "like" the page or "join the group" so they get updated whenever you post something on Facebook.

Of course, you can't post confidential or classified data, but you can post helpful information on the page to remind soldiers about upcoming events and deadlines.

SUMMARY:

Family Readiness affects unit readiness. When you're deployed, the last thing you need to worry about is the well-being of your family. If you know your family is taken care of and has a support channel, you will be more effective with your job.

Company Commanders must ensure FRGs are established, resourced and functional. If your unit doesn't have one, you need to make it a top priority to get one in place.

Part Four
Effective Leadership

Chapter 19

Your Ultimate Purpose

If you only remember one thing from this entire book, remember this: <u>Your ultimate job as the Company Commander is to ensure your unit and soldiers are prepared for war.</u>

Let me repeat that again. **Your ultimate job as the Company Commander is to ensure your unit and soldiers are prepared for war.**

Although you wear many different hats as the Company Commander, your "training your soldiers for war" hat is the most important one.

Everything you do should have some type of positive impact towards your ultimate purpose. All scheduled training, all meetings, physical fitness events, and so forth, should in some way or another PREPARE your troops for combat. If it doesn't, you're not doing your job right.

How do you ensure your troops are prepared for war? That's a good question.

Training your soldiers for combat is a PROCESS, NOT A DESTINATION. In other words, you'll never really arrive. You'll simply improve with each training event.

Over time, your small incremental improvements can result in an astronomical difference.

There are a few things you will need to do:

1) Develop and Assess the Unit METL

2) Conduct Warrior Task Training (formerly Common Task Training)

3) Instill and Maintain Discipline

4) Maintain a High Level of Unit Physical Fitness

5) Sustain and Improve Weapons Proficiency

6) Ensure Soldiers are MOS Proficient

7) Plan, Conduct, and Assess Collective Training

8) Maintain Family Readiness

9) Maintain Soldier Readiness

Let's take a few moments and cover each of these areas in a little more detail.

Develop and Assess a Unit METL

One of your first priorities after taking command is to submit a proposed Mission Essential Task Listing (METL) to your Battalion Commander for approval. Your METL tasks are the mission essential tasks your unit must be able to complete as a unit, in order to accomplish its wartime mission.

To get started, you can review the previous commander's METL. You should also reference the pertinent ARTEP or do a quick Internet search. If that doesn't help, talk with a few of your Company Commander peers and have them give you a copy of their unit METL.

Once you review these resources, your job is to draft/prepare a proposed METL, which identifies the critical, mission-essential tasks. More than likely, you will identify 4-5 tasks.

Once you identify the tasks, review them with your First Sergeant, Company XO, and Platoon Leaders. Seek their input.

Once that is complete, draft up a formal Memorandum for Record and submit it to the Battalion S3 and Battalion Commander for approval.

Once your METL is approved, share it with everyone in your company. Everyone should know what the "mission essential" tasks are. Hand out fliers, post your METL on the bulletin board and talk about it whenever you can.

Your METL assessment is broken down into "T" for trained, "P" for proficient, and "U" for untrained.

More than likely, your unit METL will consist mostly of "Ps" and "Us" at the beginning of your time in command. Your objective is to obtain a minimum "P" in each METL task. You can only obtain "Ts" when you are evaluated by a command two units higher (typically your Brigade HQs).

Whenever your unit conducts collective training you MUST EVALUATE and ASSESS the training.

Remember, your job is not to look pretty on paper. Instead, your job is to obtain an honest and accurate assessment of your unit, and then find ways to IMPROVE.

It's better to give an honest assessment and have a "U" than to finger-jam a "P" onto your assessment.

As you identify shortcomings, you must PLAN collective training in areas your unit needs to improve upon. You must also maintain your proficiency with the other METL tasks.

You should update your METL every time your unit conducts collective training. Finally, ALL scheduled training should support METL tasks.

Conduct Warrior Task Training

Warrior Task Training, formerly known as Common Task Training is the cornerstone of unit training.

In essence, collective training is a series of Warrior Tasks and MOS skills, conducted by a Squad sized element or larger. In other words, if your soldier cannot perform their individual tasks, your platoons and company will not be able to perform their collective tasks.

Examples of warrior tasks include:

- Engage Targets with M2
- Engage Targets with MK 19
- Employ Mines and Hand Grenades
- Perform Voice Communications (SITREP, SPOTREP, etc.)

It's important to remember that <u>most warrior tasks are perishable skills</u>. If you don't train and retrain on these tasks frequently, your soldiers will forget how to do them.

The best way to overcome this problem is to identify the MOST IMPORTANT warrior tasks that make up your unit's collective tasks and conduct training on those tasks every 90-days.

Instill and Maintain Discipline

As I see it, <u>discipline is the most important thing for a unit to be successful</u>. Without discipline, nothing else really matters.

Your job as the leader is to set a good example AND instill discipline in your unit. What does this mean?

Basically, you need to publish STANDARDS, the Army standards, and then you need to enforce those standards equally to everyone in your unit.

Soldiers need to know what is expected of them at all times and what the consequences are if they fail to meet the standards.

When something is wrong, you need to address it and fix it immediately. You need to be accountable to the standards yourself and you need to make sure that everyone else follows them as well.

This means that soldiers salute, stand at parade rest and render the proper military customs and courtesies. It means that soldiers are in the right uniform. It means that traditions, customs and courtesies are honored. It means that disrespect and laziness are never tolerated.

Maintain a High level of Physical Fitness

Combat is strenuous. When you deploy overseas, you will work long hours and perform strenuous labor. That is why the Army stresses physical fitness.

I already mentioned this previously, but you must maintain your physical fitness personally and you must ensure your soldiers stay fit.

When possible, implement physical fitness training in all training events. Make sure your soldiers take an APFT. If they fail the test, hold them accountable AND help them improve.

Every month, schedule PT at the beginning or end of every Saturday and Sunday. Add it to your training schedule and show your soldiers that it is a top priority for you.

Sustain and Improve Weapons Proficiency

Soldiers must be able to shoot, move and communicate. Weapons proficiency is vital.

In combat, soldiers must be able to kill the enemy and defend themselves. The only way to become proficient with anything is to practice.

Schedule ranges. Go to the field. Utilize the EST 2000, if available. Strive to shoot two to three times per year, not just a once-a-year weapons qualification.

Conduct platoon and company level "defense" training. Set up an Area of Operations and have another unit "attack." Use MILES Gear for realistic training.

Upon completion of the exercise, assess the event. Conduct an AAR with your unit and talk about the lessons learned.

Do whatever it takes to make sure your soldiers are proficient with their assigned weapon.

Ensure Soldiers are MOS Proficient

You must conduct tough, realistic MOS training. Your soldiers must be MOS proficient, prior to deploying overseas. Obviously, they must be MOSQ, but more importantly, they must also know their job.

If you have mechanics, for example, they must know how to change a transmission, do an oil change, change a tire, conduct recovery ops, etc.

Always monitor your MOSQ rate. Send your soldiers to MOSQ School, if they are not qualified for their current duty position.

Also, make sure Platoon Sergeants are conducting Squad and Platoon Level MOS training.

Remember, **individual training is tied to collective training.**

The only way your company can complete its tasks is if each individual soldier, each squad, and each platoon can accomplish their tasks.

It would also be in your best interest to <u>ensure your soldiers are cross-trained</u>. Have each platoon in your company cross-train with other soldiers in their platoon.

For example, have the fuelers in your distribution platoon train with the ammo handlers and the cooks. This gives each soldier added skills and also improves your unit's ability to get things done.

Plan, Conduct, and Assess Collective Training

We covered this earlier, too. Plan tough, realistic training.

Officers plan training. NCOs execute training. Officers are responsible for collective training and NCOs handle individual training. Your unit must train collectively.

Get out of the armory and go to an installation or training area. Set-up your equipment, a command post, an area of operations and train.

Train as you would in combat. Wear full battle rattle. Make your soldiers carry their weapons with them.

Do everything tactically. Plan each training exercise. Resource it properly. Conduct training. Evaluate training. Do an AAR and repeat the process each drill-weekend.

Maintain Family Readiness

Your unit is a family. You must take care of each other. That means taking care of your soldiers' families, too.

The secret to success is communication. Soldiers and their families must know what is going on at all times. Shared information (if allowed) is more valuable than hoarded information.

If you have information that isn't classified or on a need to know basis, share it with your soldiers and their families. Let them know what is going on!

Establish an FRG. Make sure your soldiers have Family Care Plans. Start a newsletter. Send it to every soldier. Send it to spouses. **Communicate.** You cannot communicate too much.

Maintain Soldier Readiness

Soldier readiness is a very important part of your job. This boils down to having your soldiers deployable, medically fit, mentally fit, and MOSQ. You need to monitor these metrics every single month on a soldier-by-soldier basis.

When a soldier becomes medically non-deployable, you need to know their status and what the game plan is to get them medically fit.

When someone goes on profile (temporary or permanent) you need to know why and have a game-plan to remedy it.

When a soldier is not MOSQ, you need to know why and you need to have a game-plan to get them MOSQ.

You also need to make sure that your soldiers are physically and mentally fit and ready to do their wartime mission.

I personally believe that if you are conducting battle focused training, most of these things should fall into place. However, keep a close eye on your key metrics and track it like a hawk.

Also, keep in mind this is NCO driven. These are the things your 1SG should be doing. Just spot check from time-to-time and see if they need help with anything.

Summary

Never forget your purpose as a Company Commander. Do whatever you can to make sure your soldiers are prepared to deploy and complete their combat mission, even at a moment's notice. Plan tough, realistic, battle focused training. Focus on getting a little bit better every month.

Chapter 20

Establishing Your Priorities

Everyone has priorities. *The easiest way to determine someone's priorities is to look at how and where they spend their time and money.*

Your priorities should dictate WHAT you do. Your priorities will dictate how much time you will spend on specific tasks. If you don't have clearly defined priorities, you will run around like a chicken with their head cut off.

You will be busy, but ineffective. You will get stressed out, burned out and wonder why nothing of importance is getting accomplished.

As a Company Commander, you must establish your priorities, BEFORE you take command.

Before we get too deep into this topic, I need to tell you something. YOU CAN'T DO IT ALL!

Commanders are ultimately responsible for everything that happens (and fails to happen) in their unit, but they can't do it all themselves.

In order to succeed as a Company Commander and use proper time-management, you need to decide what's MOST important to you. To do so, you need to establish priorities for your unit, your direct reports, and for yourself. I'll cover more on each topic in the paragraphs below.

Unit Priorities

One of your first key objectives as the new commander is to establish your unit priorities. In other words, what are the most important things your unit must accomplish, in order to be successful?

In my unit, our unit priorities were:

1. Strength Management

2. Training

3. Unit Readiness

I established these priorities <u>PRIOR</u> to taking command. I did so by assessing the unit, talking with key leaders, and establishing a VISION for what I wanted the unit to look like.

You may ask why I put strength management first. Obviously, training is more important.

I realized we couldn't conduct worthwhile collective training, with less than half of our authorized strength currently on hand.

Therefore, we would need to recruit new soldiers and retain the ones we had. That took precedence over training. Each organization is different.

I wouldn't expect you to have the same exact priorities we did, or in the same exact order. It's possible, but highly unlikely.

What's most important is that you establish priorities based upon YOUR assessment of your organization.

Once you establish unit priorities, you must share them with your leaders and soldiers. Post them on the unit bulletin board and brief your soldiers. Do whatever it takes so that EVERYONE in your organization understands what's most important.

Personal Priorities

Once you have established unit priorities, you must identify your personal priorities, as the Company Commander.

My priorities were:

- Mission Planning
- Collective Training
- Leader Development

These three priorities were things that I focused my personal energy and efforts on. These three areas consumed most of my time. Practically everything else was delegated to someone else.

Remember, you can't do it all. You must ask yourself, what are the most important things I should do? What activities should I do that will have the greatest positive impact on my organization? How should I spend my time?

You may have different personal priorities than I did. Your organization is different than mine. You have different strengths and weaknesses, too. That's okay.

Just remember to choose YOUR Big three, and focus on those things first.

Whenever you get tasked to do something or find something that needs to be done, ask yourself if it is one of your Big 3. If it's not, delegate it to one of your key leaders.

Some examples of Company Commander priorities might include:

- Discipline
- Collective Training
- Morale
- Soldier Recognition
- Maintenance
- Property Accountability
- Retention
- Leader Development
- Unit Readiness

Like I stated before, all of these things are important, but that doesn't mean that you have to do them personally.

Before you take command (or as soon as you get command), draft up your own list of priorities. Talk with the outgoing Company Commander. Ask them what are the strengths of the organization? What were their priorities?

Also, talk with the First Sergeant and Company XO to see what their priorities are. Chances are they've never clearly identified them.

Your Key Leaders' Priorities

We're making great progress so far. We've established your unit priorities and your personal priorities.

What I'm going to say next may contradict some things you've already been taught.

<u>Everyone's priorities must support the unit's priorities; however, your First Sergeant, Company XO and AGR Staff should NOT have the same priorities as you do.</u>

If you want an efficient, effective and excellent company, you must talk with and mentor your First Sergeant, Company XO, Platoon Leaders and AGR Staff. You must help each of them establish their Big 3.

For instance, your Company XO could choose from any of the following priorities:

- Unit Maintenance
- Administration
- Supply
- Reports & Suspenses
- Awards and Evaluations

As the leader of the organization, you should set their priorities for them.

You should counsel and mentor them, discussing the unit priorities and sharing your personal priorities.

Once you've done this, you can assign them priorities, based upon the things that they can do best.

Listed below, I have provided an example of the Big 3 for each key leader within an Army National Guard or Army Reserve company.

Commander Priorities

- Mission Planning
- Leader Development
- Morale & Soldier Recognition

First Sergeant Priorities

- Warrior Task Training
- Enlisted Promotion System
- Unit Discipline

Company XO Priorities

- Unit Maintenance
- Command Supply Discipline Program
- Suspenses

Readiness NCO Priorities

- Military Pay
- Unit Administration
- Reports

<u>Training NCO Priorities</u>

- Manage ATTRS
- Resource Unit Training
- Ensure Soldiers are prepared for military schools

<u>Supply NCO Priorities</u>

- Oversee Inventories
- Order Supplies
- Property Accountability

<u>Admin NCO</u>

- Processing Administrative Paperwork
- Update Files in IPERMS
- Manage Unit Files

Conclusion

Remember, <u>everyone has priorities</u>. Unfortunately, most people don't know what their own priorities should be. They attempt to do everything themselves and end up accomplishing very little.

If you want to succeed as a Company Commander, you must first establish unit priorities; the Big 3. Next, you must identify your personal Big 3 priorities. Finally, you must sit down with each of your key leaders and AGR Staff and assign each person a Big 3.

Once everyone knows what their priorities are, people can "stay in their lane." In addition, team-members will find themselves more efficient and more effective because they are only focusing of a few key things.

Chapter 21

Effective Time Management

<u>Time is our most precious asset</u>. It's the only thing we can't get more of. I'm sure you already realize that.

As an ARNG or USAR Company Commander you are working on a compressed time schedule, so you have to be very disciplined with your time.

What I want to do in the paragraphs below is share a few time management tips that helped me out during my time in Company Command. These tips are listed in no particular order.

1 The 20/80 Rule

You've probably heard of the Pareto Principle before. It's not a new concept. Basically, the rule states that 20 percent of the things you do produce 80 percent of the results.

I will take it a step further and tell you that 20 percent of your soldiers will produce 80 percent of the problems. And 20 percent of your soldiers will do 80 percent of the work.

The real takeaway here is that a small group of tasks (and people) will give you the biggest bang for the buck and produce the best results.

Make sure that you spend a majority of your time on the few critical tasks you need to do to be successful.

Spend 80 percent of your time on the top 20 percent, most important tasks. Spend 80 percent of your time mentoring the top 20 percent of your soldiers.

2 Establish Priorities

In the previous chapter we talked about priorities. I just want to remind you that you need clear priorities. Every single day, during drill weekend, and outside of drill weekend, you should know what your two to three most critical tasks for that day are. Always put the first things first.

3 Don't Confuse Being Busy with Being Productive

Everyone I know is busy, yet few people are really productive. Most people waste a lot of time during a typical work day, sometimes without even realizing it.

Don't think that checking emails, surfing the internet and having meetings are the best use of your time.

Everything you do should be based upon the impact it has on your unit. Being busy is the sign of the average leader. Being productive is the sign of the great leader.

4 Delegate

This was one of the hardest lessons I had to learn during my military career. I am naturally a doer and enjoy getting things done.

As a leader, you must realize that *the Army pays you to get things done through other people.*

You have a support staff for a reason. Leverage them. You can't do everything yourself anyway.

I would argue that if you are given a task and it isn't one of your Big 3 priorities, you should delegate it to someone else. The sooner you learn how to delegate, the better off you will be!

If someone else can do a task even 75% as well as you can, delegate it. Besides, your subordinates want to be empowered and challenged.

As a quick reminder, <u>you can't delegate your responsibility, but you can delegate the task at hand.</u>

5 Keep Meetings to a Minimum

I hate meetings. Most Army meetings are extremely unproductive. They do nothing but waste people's time.

Many people are in the habit of having meetings just to have a meeting (or to hear themselves talk).

As the Company Commander, keep your meetings to a bare-bones minimum. Make sure that every meeting you do have is well thought out.

Have an agenda for every meeting. Rehearse ahead of time. Spend some time to determine who actually needs to attend your meeting. Whatever you do, keep ALL of your meetings to 60-minutes or less.

6 Plan Out Your Day

One of the things that helped me be productive as a Company Commander was to plan out my day.

You already have access to the training schedule and Yearly Training Calendar, so this should be pretty easy to do.

Each day of drill weekend, you want to have your day planned out in 15-minute increments.

The first thing you want to do is get a day planner. Once you do that, schedule in the most important activities of the day.

<u>Determine WHEN you will do each activity</u>. Set time limits. After you've scheduled in all of the big things first, then you can schedule in everything else that needs to be done.

The Most Important Question

The single most important question you can ask yourself is this: **"Is what I'm working on right now the BEST use of my time?"**

I've found that if you ask yourself that question every time you start a new project or task, it will help you decide whether or not you should focus on that or something else.

Final Thoughts

The bottom line is that you will always be challenged for time.

USAR and ARNG Company Commanders have two days a month to do what Active Duty Company Commanders have 30-days to do. The only way to be successful is to manage your time wisely.

Follow the tips mentioned in this chapter and you should be well on your way.

Chapter 22

Developing Leaders

Other than training your unit for its wartime mission, <u>developing your subordinate leaders is your second biggest responsibility.</u>

Unfortunately, most Army Reserve and National Guard officers do not get the same leadership experience as Active Duty Army officers.

While Active Duty officers lead their soldiers day-in-and-day-out, National Guard and Army Reserve officers are limited to IDT weekend and Annual Training.

Before I get too deep on this topic, let me clarify one thing.

I'm not saying Active Duty Officers are better leaders than Army Reserve or National Guard Officers. Instead, I'm saying that Active Duty Officers get more military experience than we do.

Experience helps people grow. <u>Evaluated experience helps people change and develop their potential.</u>

It's difficult to develop your own leadership skills, if you don't get much experience. More importantly, it's hard to develop or teach your subordinates, if you barely know what you're doing yourself.

One of the biggest challenges I've had was trying to develop my senior NCOs and officers.

Let's be brutally honest for a moment. For the most part, you'll only have your soldiers with you two days per month and for a couple of weeks during Annual Training.

It's hard to effectively develop people when you only work with them two or three days per month. Therefore, you must develop a written game-plan covering who you will develop, what you will teach them and how you will do it.

Without a plan, you're setting yourself up for failure.

Who Should You Develop?

At a minimum, you should develop your Company XO, Platoon Leaders and your First Sergeant.

You should teach your Company XO how to be an XO and more importantly, how to be a Company Commander. One day your Company XO will be a Company Commander and hopefully you'll have helped train them properly.

Next, you should mentor your Platoon Leaders. One of the greatest ways to mentor your Platoon Leaders is to get them joined at the hip with their Platoon Sergeant.

Ultimately, your NCOs will help form the leadership foundation of your Platoon Leaders. In addition, you can utilize your Company XO to help teach your Platoon Leaders.

Finally, you can be a good example for them to follow. Remember that everyone is watching you. Lead from the front and inspire people by your own actions.

Some folks might be wondering how a Company Commander can mentor their First Sergeant considering the 1SG typically has a lot more life experience and military experience than the Company Commander does.

<u>We can all learn from each other</u>. As the commander, you can mentor your First Sergeant by teaching them new things about mission planning, building a successful team, setting goals, and professional development.

Lead by example and show them what a squared away Company Commander looks like.

Probably the best thing you can do is build a good working relationship with them, based upon sound communication, loyalty and trust.

In most cases, the 1SG will mentor you more than you mentor them, but you should still do what you can to share your knowledge and experience with them to help make them a better leader.

What Should You Teach Them?

Officers should be technically and tactically proficient. In addition, they must possess and continue to develop:

- Communication Skills
- Leadership skills
- People skills

The most valuable lesson you can teach your officers is "self-discovery." Help them discover their own strengths, weaknesses, leadership styles, personality, etc.

I've discovered several books that really helped me teach my subordinates (please see the resources section at the end of this book for a complete reading list).

Utilize the Myers-Brigg® personality test to identify each person's personality. Have your subordinates take the "strengths-finder" quiz in the book, "Now Discover Your Strengths," by Marcus Buckingham. That quiz is life-changing.

Another great way to teach your officers is to have a "Company Commander for the day" program during drill weekend. Each month or every other month, during drill weekend, let one of your subordinate's job shadow with you.

Let them attend battalion meetings with you. Have them run company meetings, prepare correspondence, make decisions, etc. Personally, I find this to be a very effective way to develop your subordinates.

One day, most of your lieutenants will be Company Commanders anyway. Give them the opportunity to see what it's like now. Even though you are still "in charge" empower them step up and take charge.

How to Do It!

I've found a couple of effective ways to develop my junior officers and NCOs.

One great method is by **establishing a reading program**. Each quarter, I choose (or my officers choose) a book to read for professional development.

After we read the book, we draft a one-page executive summary and then had a discussion to share what we've learned.

Another great way to develop your subordinates is to watch a movie together. Pick a good military history movie. Next, assign each officer a different movie character. Have one officer be the Battalion Commander, the Company Commander, the First Sergeant (different leaders in the movie).

At the end of the movie, have a group discussion about what each character did right, what they did wrong and most importantly, how they could have handled things differently. Talk about the key lessons learned from the movie.

Next, make sure that you lead by example at all times. One of the best ways to mentor others is to set a good example for them to follow. This means that you are a professional at all times, you keep a good attitude, you stay in shape, you live the Warrior Ethos and promote the Army values.

You have to remember that your followers are always watching you and many of them will do what you do, so make sure you set a good example.

Finally, counseling is the best way to develop your subordinates. The best counseling is face-to-face, one-on-one via a two-way conversation.

As the counselor, you should mostly ask questions and listen. If you're doing all the talking, it's not really counseling; it's a lecture. Help them answer their own questions and solve their own problems.

Obviously, if you are counseling for poor performance or a discipline issue, you will do things differently.

Summary

Developing your leaders should be one of your top priorities. Make sure you set aside at least four hours every drill weekend to develop your subordinates. I know it's a lot of work, but it's also a big part of your job.

Chapter 23

Soldier Recognition

One of your biggest responsibilities as a leader is soldier recognition. **Soldiers deserve to be recognized for their contributions.** You must find creative ways to recognize your good soldiers, and even recognize your average soldiers when they do something great.

I can tell you that "not feeling appreciated" is one of the major causes of soldiers leaving the Army, bad morale and poor performance. And one of the best ways to fix that problem is to recognize the people who work for you.

There are many effective ways to recognize your soldiers. The Army Reserve and Army National Guard offer a wide variety of incentives such as:

- Medals
- Certificate of Appreciate
- Company or Battalion Coin
- Soldier of the Month
- Schools (e.g. Airborne, Air Assault)
- Praise
- Thank You Cards

What I want to do in the paragraphs below is cover each type of recognition in greater detail.

Medals

Medals were created to be awarded. It costs you NOTHING to submit someone for an achievement medal (just a little bit of time). In addition, the Army has different medals for different achievements.

Some people have the mindset that medals should be awarded sparingly. I disagree. I don't think you should hand them out like candy at Halloween, but I do not see a problem with awarding several achievement medals each drill weekend.

<u>Your job is to look for soldiers going above and beyond what is expected of them, and submit them for awards.</u>

In addition to the Army Achievement Medal and Army Commendation Medal, there are also state medals (for National Guard personnel). Learn more about these medals and find out what your Battalion Commander's policy is for awards.

Throughout my time in command, I tried to submit at least three soldiers for achievement medals each drill weekend. As a result, we were constantly recognizing soldiers. It had a HUGE impact on morale and performance.

In addition, I never felt the awards were watered down because we did this. Remember, your soldiers are almost ALWAYS doing something good. It's your job to notice and reward the good behavior.

To the best of my knowledge, I have NEVER heard of anyone turning down a medal. Have you? Soldiers are proud to earn medals and it's your job to help them do that.

Not only will medals impact morale and performance, but it will also give your soldiers additional promotion points! Talk about a win-win situation.

Certificates of Achievement/Appreciation

If you don't already have a Company Certificate of Appreciation or Achievement, get one.

Talk to your soldiers and find out who has excellent drawing skills. Create a contest and have some of your soldiers submit their drawings. Select the best one and put it on your Company COA.

Another key point to remember is that COAs with a LTC signature or higher, are worth promotion points for your soldiers.

Rather than submit all your soldiers for a Company COA, select the top two or three soldiers each month and submit them for a Battalion COA.

Why not get your soldiers additional promotion points if you can?

Unit Coins

Another great way to recognize soldiers is to create a unit coin.

Traditionally, most battalions and higher have unit coins. Most companies do not.

I'd encourage you to create a customized unit coin. Conduct an Internet search and find some different companies that make Challenge Coins.

You should be able to get your first order of 100 coins, including set-up fees, for about $500 or less. If needed, conduct a unit fundraiser to help pay for the coins. Or, ask the 1SG to go in half with you.

Teach your soldiers about the history of Army Challenge Coins. Teach them how to "challenge" others. For instance, if you received a coin in the past and someone challenges you, you must present your coin or pay a consequence. You could do push-ups; buy that person a soda or beer, or some other creative method.

I can't speak for anyone else, but the coins I've earned during my career have just as much value to me as the medals I earned. Trust me, your soldiers will appreciate receiving a unit coin for doing a great job!

Soldier of the Month

You should talk with your First Sergeant about creating a Company Soldier of the Month program, if there isn't one already in place.

Each IDT weekend, you should set aside an hour (before or after scheduled training) and conduct your SOM board. It can be formal or informal. This is a wonderful way to recognize soldiers.

Schools (i.e. Airborne, Air Assault, etc.)

Sending your high-speed soldiers to military schools is a great way to recognize your soldiers. You should talk with your Readiness NCO and S3 about acquiring slots for Airborne and Air Assault schools for your company, at a minimum.

You should send your best soldiers to these schools.

Use the school as an incentive. Let your soldiers know that if they do the right thing and do it well, they will be rewarded. Specialty schools are great for soldier development. They also improve morale, esprit-de-corps and unit readiness.

Praise

Most soldiers appreciate honest and sincere praise more than anything else.

When one of your soldiers does something outstanding, bring them to the front of your formation and talk about it. Let your other soldiers know about that soldier's accomplishments.

Remember, ALWAYS PRAISE IN PUBLIC! Make a point to tell your soldiers they did a good job when others are around. Be as specific as possible when you praise them.

One of the things we did at my unit was to bring new soldiers to the front of the formation and introduce them to the entire company. It worked very well.

When soldiers are about to leave your unit (retirement, ETS, promotion, transfer, etc.) bring them to the front of formation and talk about them.

Tell your unit what you admire most about that person, funny things they said or did, and talk about how they contributed to your organization.

Ask your soldiers to give input and tell what they will remember most about that person.

One key point to remember is that <u>people like to be recognized in different ways</u>. Believe it or not, not everyone likes to receive a medal in front of the entire company. While some people do, others simply want an "atta-boy" or a pat on the back.

It's your job to find out HOW your soldiers want to be recognized. One way to find out is to simply ASK your soldiers "what motivates you?" or "how do you like to be recognized?" Your soldiers will tell you what makes them tick.

Thank You Cards

When I took command, I had some stationary made up with my name and rank on it. At the end of every drill weekend I personally hand wrote five thank you cards to soldiers that did a great job during drill weekend.

Every drill weekend, soldiers would approach me and thank me for writing them a thank you card the month before. They told me I was their first leader to ever do this for them.

I incorporated this idea into my leadership philosophy because during my 15+ years in the military, I only received two hand-written thank you cards from my superiors. I treasure those two cards more than any award I ever received. I know how effective a hand-written note can be.

The moral of the story is to get some nice stationary made up and send a few handwritten thank you cards after every drill weekend. This alone will have a huge impact on morale.

What to Reward Soldiers for?

At this point, you might be wondering, what should I reward soldiers for? That is a great question and I'll give you some examples of things to look for. Here are a few things that come to mind.

1. Qualifying Expert with their assigned weapon

2. Graduating a military school as an Honor Grad or the Distinguished Grad

3. Scoring a 270 or higher on the APFT

4. Completing a duty or job above their pay-grade

5. Doing anything significant to help out another soldier

6. Writing or developing a unit SOP

7. Performing an additional duty to a high standard

8. Receiving a high score during an inspection

9. Doing anything to save the unit money or time

10. Reorganizing an office or building

11. Solving any type of problem the unit is experiencing

12. Mentoring and developing others

13. Improving morale in the unit

14. Encouraging and motivating others to reenlist

15. Helping the unit win any type of contest or competition

Just to clarify, I'm not saying you have to award a soldier a medal for accomplishing any of these things, but these achievements all deserve some type of recognition. Ultimately, what you decide to recognize people for (and how you do it) is totally up to you.

Summary

In summary, it's your job to recognize your soldiers. As I see it, no soldier should ever leave your unit without some type of recognition, such as a coin, medal, plaque or certificate. No soldier should ever retire and not get a medal for their service.

One of your key responsibilities as the Company Commander is to ensure your soldiers are recognized and rewarded for their ongoing achievements.

If you keep your eyes and ears open, you will find plenty of things to recognize.

Chapter 24

How to Conduct a Meeting

Personally, <u>I HATE meetings</u>. No, I take that back; I hate inefficient, unproductive meetings that waste my time.

Although meetings are a necessary evil, most meetings do more bad than good. Most meetings accomplish NOTHING.

Have you ever participated in a meeting that lasted 3 or 4-hours? Have you ever sat in on a meeting and asked yourself WHY am I here?

Have you ever day-dreamed, fell asleep, or spent the entire meeting thinking about something else? Have you ever left a meeting wondering what you accomplished?

If you answered YES to any of the above questions, you understand what it's like to attend an ineffective meeting. Ineffective meetings are a waste of time and money.

Ineffective meetings are ineffective for one or more of the following reasons: (1) no purpose, (2) no agenda, (3) wrong attendees, and (4) not ran properly.

Effective meetings must have a <u>SPECIFIC</u> purpose. Without a crystal clear, specific purpose, there's no point having a meeting in the first place.

Furthermore, effective meetings have agendas AND have the right attendees in the audience.

Once you know the purpose of your meeting, you need to draft and finalize an agenda and decide who REALLY needs to attend.

Finally, facilitators must run their meetings efficiently by following a time schedule and keeping attendees focused.

As the Company Commander, you will attend most battalion meetings and some brigade level meetings. In addition, you will host your own company meetings. Although you can't control how your battalion or brigade operates their meetings, you can control how you run yours.

Listed below, I want to give you some tips on how to conduct a meeting the right way.

Preparing for a Meeting

When you decide a meeting is necessary (clear purpose), you must take a few minutes and plan your meeting. It's similar to following the 1/3 – 2/3 rule for mission planning.

Take a few minutes, sit down and draft up a purpose and agenda. Once you draft up an agenda, put it down for an hour or two and then come back and review it and eliminate any information that does not correspond with the real PURPOSE of that meeting.

Once your agenda is finalized, decide who needs to attend. In other words, do both the Platoon Sergeants and Platoon Leaders need to attend? Do your XO and First Sergeant both need to be there?

Next, set the time for the meeting. After that's done, notify the participants and tell them what the purpose of the meeting is, what they will need to bring, and what you will expect them to know/brief at the meeting.

When you have your monthly Training and Command & Staff meetings, please keep in mind that most of your NCOs and officers will have to travel from their civilian jobs to attend.

Try to set the time for the meeting outside of normal work hours so they have enough time to prepare. Also, keep in mind that your soldiers have civilian jobs to report back to the following day, so don't have your meetings late at night either.

In our unit we had our meetings at 1800 hours.

Knowing what I know right now, I would recommend meetings start at 1845 or 1900 hours during the week.

Meeting Checklist

- Decide the purpose of your meeting
- Draft a proposed agenda
- Revise and finalize the agenda
- Determine who needs to attend
- Determine what information attendees will need to know/brief
- Set time for meeting
- Notify attendees of meeting
- Conduct the Meeting within 60-minutes
- Finish the meeting and conduct the back-brief

- Schedule a follow up meeting if the meeting can't be finished in 60-minutes

Conducting the Meeting

Since you took the time to adequately prepare for your meeting, you have increased your chances of success. Although preparation is vital, so is the actual execution of your meeting.

Once you set a specific time for your meeting to start, start on time. If your meeting is scheduled for 1845 hours, don't start at 1846 hours. Even if people are running late, start your meeting on time.

<u>When you start your meeting on time, your soldiers will know that you value their time</u>. They will know that you are serious and they will respect you for it.

On the other hand, if you start late, you will lose credibility. Your soldiers will think it is okay to be a few minutes late, because you never start on time anyway.

If soldiers arrive late, pull them aside after the meeting and tell them you will not tolerate tardiness. Put it in writing on a counseling statement, if necessary

Now that you've started your meeting on time, the next process is to open your meeting the right way.

When I open a meeting, I take roll call and then I inform the attendees of the purpose (what we are trying to accomplish), and the time limit for the meeting. We also review the agenda and I ask if anyone has any questions, before we get started.

Listed below is an example of how I open the meeting:

"Hello. It's nice to see all of you again. Tonight, we will conduct our monthly training meeting and command and staff meeting. The purpose of our meeting is to review last month's training, discuss this month's training, and review future training (120-days out). Once the training meeting is finished, we will immediately begin our command and staff meeting.

When our meeting is finished, we will all have a clear understanding about last month's training, this month's training and we should clearly understand the mission and responsibilities of each person in attendance. We have 60-minutes to complete both meetings. Are there any questions before we begin?"

Once the meeting starts, you need to follow the agenda. As the facilitator, your job is to keep side bar at a minimum and keep people focused and on track.

Some people like to talk a lot, and they will tend to ramble. If you don't keep them focused and on track, your meetings can last hours.

As you move through the agenda, keep a close eye on the clock. Have time limits identified for each area on the agenda. Know when you are on schedule, ahead of schedule or behind schedule.

Concluding the Meeting

Once the meeting is finished, you <u>MUST</u> conduct a back-brief with your attendees. In other words, have each person brief you on what they took away from the meeting. Have them explain to you what they believe is expected of them.

You can have a smooth, fast-paced meeting, but, if attendees don't digest the pertinent information, your meeting was not successful. The best way to ensure your soldiers take away the key points is to have them take notes AND conduct a back-brief with you, immediately after the meeting.

Conclusion

In summary, <u>meetings are a necessary evil</u>. As a Company Commander, your job is to adequately prepare for meetings AND to run your meetings efficiently.

To do so, use an agenda, invite your target audience, keep your meetings to 60-minutes or less, and conduct a back-brief immediately after the meeting. Good luck!

Part Five
Leaving a Legacy

Chapter 25

Taking Your Organization to the Next level

All Company Commanders should strive to improve their organization. I refer to this as the 3 E's. I mentioned it earlier, but we will cover it in a little more detail now.

The three E's stand for Effective, Efficient and Excellent. The 3 E's are a process. Before you can create an efficient or excellent organization, you must first become effective.

EFFECTIVE:

Can your unit get the job done? Can they complete any task, or just about any task? Can your Battalion Commander count on your company? When the battalion has an important mission, do they give the mission to your company?

In my opinion, being effective starts with the right mind-set. It's not a "that's not my job mentality." Instead, it's having a "can-do" attitude.

It also entails being good at your unit mission and individual tasks. One of my former Battalion Commanders instilled a "just get it done mentality" into every officer in his organization. He taught us that the mission comes first.

Whether a particular task is in your job description or not, is irrelevant. Your job is to get it done or find someone to get it done.

While I was in Company Command, my company was a Forward Support Company. We supported an Infantry Battalion.

From day one, I instilled into my soldiers that "everything we do is about the war-fighter," aka the infantryman.

Our personal agendas cannot take priority over our unit's agenda.

This "mind-set" or "attitude" was adopted throughout the organization. As a result, we became very effective at getting our job done. Everything we did was about supporting the war-fighter and making their life easier.

<u>We realized the war-fighter was our customer and our job was to provide world-class customer service.</u>

Remember, Company Commander, everything starts with you. Whatever you deem is important, your officers, NCOs and soldiers will accept as important.

If you can create a winning environment by placing the mission first, you will have a very effective organization.

What are some things you can do to determine if your unit is effective?

Here are a few questions to ask yourself.

- Do we follow the training schedule?
- Are we good at getting things done?
- Can my boss count on my unit?
- Do we complete tasks on time and to standard?

- Are we reliable?

- Do we provide good customer service to the units we support?

- Can we accomplish our wartime mission?

I understand your unit is a work in progress. That's okay. Strive to get a little bit better every single day. It all starts with the right attitude.

EFFICIENT:

I've always been a hard-worker. I've also known people who work long hours, in attempt to get the mission done, or to impress their boss.

Anyone can work long hours, and many people do, but the secret is to be efficient at what you do.

As a Company Commander, you have limited time and limited resources. You must ensure the mission gets done on time and to standard.

In my opinion, part of your planning process should also include "finding the best way to get the job done." You must utilize your soldiers and resources effectively. When you have a task, you must determine how to allocate those resources.

In addition, you might have several different missions going on at the same time. For instance, you might have support missions at three different locations. You will need to come up with a game-plan to complete all three missions in the most effective way.

How do you create an efficient organization? I find it fairly simple. First of all, identify your "go-to" people. In any organization, there are what I call "clutch" people. These are the people you can always count on.

It's similar to Pareto's 20/80 rule, which states 20 percent of your people accomplish 80 percent of the work. Utilize these 20 percent and put them in charge of projects. Sometimes these folks are the highest-ranking folks and sometimes they aren't.

Just know who your "studs" are, and give them a chance to shine.

Another way to improve efficiency is to establish what are known as "Best Practices." When you find a great way to do something, write it down, and incorporate it into one of your SOPs. **Establish benchmarks and set high standards for everyone in your organization.**

Finally, a third way to increase efficiency in your organization is to ask your subordinate officers, NCOs and soldiers for their input. Utilize their experience.

If you want to learn the "easiest" way to do something, ask a "lazy person" in your organization. They will probably know the easiest way to do something.

Those are just three ways to be me more efficient.

EXCELLENT:

Once your company is effective and efficient, you should strive to be EXCELLENT. Excellence is an attitude. It's a sense of pride. It all starts with the Company Commander, too.

I've found that no one wants to be on a losing team. No one wants to spend their life on a 0-16 Junior Varsity team. On the other hand, everyone wants to be on the undefeated state championship, varsity team.

One of the reasons people join the military is to be part of something greater than themselves. You must create an atmosphere where people can win!

To create an excellent organization, you must:

- Clearly articulate your unit's purpose
- Reward good behavior
- Reprimand poor performance and bad behavior
- Empower your subordinates
- Create a winning atmosphere

Let's briefly cover each one.

CLEARLY ARTICULATE YOUR UNIT'S PURPOSE:

From day one of your time in command, and every day afterward, you must articulate your unit's mission to your soldiers.

Everyone should know the unit's mission and why the unit exists. They should also know how their job/role fits into that purpose.

REWARD GOOD BEHAVIOR:

Every unit has superstars. Every unit has soldiers that can be counted on. Every unit has soldiers who accomplish great things. *Your job is to recognize good behavior.*

Submit soldiers for achievement medals, COAs, Letters of Appreciation, unit coins, and more.

Promote them. Send them to schools. Hand out unit coins. Recognize the "Soldier of the Month." Find creative ways to let your soldiers know you notice their "good behavior."

REPRIMAND POOR PERFORMANCE AND BAD BEHAVIOR:

One of the worst things you can do is do nothing when soldiers mess up. When a soldier fails to meet the standards, counsel them. You should always punish/reprimand poor behavior.

If you see something wrong, make an on-the-spot correction and fix it immediately. Do not tolerate poor performance.

Put things in writing. If you need to do a personnel action, such as initiate a FLAG, a Bar to Reenlistment, or an Administrative Reduction, do it.

Your soldiers are always watching you and sometimes testing you. If you say you're going to do something, do it. Don't wait three months to do it either. On-the-spot corrections are much more effective.

Speaking from personal experience, I can tell you that there are very few things that destroy motivation more than seeing a slacker get over. When that happens, it's a slap in the face to everyone who is doing a good job.

EMPOWER YOUR SUBORDINATES:

Whenever possible, delegate tasks to your subordinates. Remember that people rise to the level of expectation that you place on them.

Entrust your followers with important tasks and missions. Let them show you what they bring to the table.

You will be absolutely amazed at what people can do when you empower them. Sure, you might get let down once in a while, but in most cases, you will be pleasantly surprised.

CREATE A WINNING ATMOSPHERE:

Like I mentioned earlier, everyone wants to be part of a winning team. Your job is to create the winning team.

In professional sports, if a team goes the entire season without winning a game, the owners fire the coach, not the players.

Remember, you are the coach. Take pride in everything you do. Share your unit's accomplishments with the Battalion Commander and with your unit's family members. Reward your soldiers in public. Create a "we are the best unit" atmosphere.

When a soldier returns home after training, they should be able to brag to their spouse and friends about how awesome training was and about how awesome their unit is.

Final Thoughts

The bottom line is that soldiers want to be part of a great organization. Your job as the leader is to set high standards; lead by example and bring out the best in your people.

Ultimately, you want an organization that is effective, efficient and excellent. This takes time to accomplish, but it's worth the energy and work.

Chapter 26

Knowing When to Leave Command

You can't and shouldn't be a Company Commander forever. Even though it's a fun and rewarding job, you still need to actively manage your own career.

In the National Guard, officers typically command for 24 to 36-months. The minimum is typically 12-months. I believe you should aim to be a Company Commander for 18 to 24-months.

Anything less than that isn't enough time in the job and anything more than that is a bit excessive (my opinion).

<u>You will not be a Captain forever</u>. Most Captains stay at that rank between 4-7 years. I believe you need to have a variety of experiences as a Captain, in order to be qualified for future promotions and job positions.

If you know that you're only going to be a Captain for 4 to 7-years, you should at a minimum have the following jobs:

- 1-2 years as a Battalion Staff Officer
- 1-2 years in command
- 1-2 years in Assistant Brigade Staff, Instructor, Aide-de-Camp, etc.

In addition, you will have your educational requirements to complete; specifically, the Captain's Career Course (typically 2 to 6-months).

If you intend on making the National Guard or Army Reserve a career, and you want to be competitive for promotion to the rank of Major, make sure you have a game-plan.

For instance, if you were a Captain for 18-months before you became a Company Commander, you know that you'll have at least another 30-months in the rank of Captain.

This helps you determine when you need certain jobs AFTER command. Remember, Captains are Captains for approximately 4 to 7-years. You cannot get promoted before the 4 years-time-in-grade anyway.

In the example above, you know you could be a Company commander for 24 to 30-months. After that, you could start searching for a Major slot or find another job to round out your Captain-level experience.

Another thing to consider is when you are a Company Commander for a long time (more than 24-months) you are holding up other people from moving into command positions.

If you've ever been held up for a position before, you know how frustrating that can be. My advice is not to do that to someone else.

Remember, if you've been in command more than 18 to 24-months and you are starting to feel burnt out, and losing your effectiveness, you need to talk with your boss and come up with a game-plan to transition to your next assignment. It's the right thing to do for your soldiers and for your own career.

Chapter 27

Life after Company Command

Is there life after Company Command? You bet. After you pass the guidon to the new Company Commander, you will experience a wide variety of emotions.

In one way, you will be sad. You might miss being a big fish in a small pond. You might miss the authority and responsibility you previously had.

You will miss your interaction with your officers, NCOs and soldiers. After all, you will probably never lead troops again; at least, not at the unit level.

On the contrary, your next job will probably be much less demanding. You will probably move into a staff position with much less responsibility.

You will have more time for your family. You will have more time for hobbies and you can have more time to relax.

I believe that outgoing Company Commanders should take some time to relax and reflect on their experience, after finishing command.

Evaluate your experience. Write some things down in your journal or memoirs. Think about all of the things that you learned during your time in command, and look for ways to improve your leadership.

You might have the desire to help the new Company Commander. Please remember, you should only do this if they ask you for advice. Never forget what it was like to be the

Company Commander. I know you didn't want the previous Company Commander stepping on your toes telling you how to do things.

In addition, the best thing you can do is break off communication with your old unit. Even though the AGR, officers and 1SG might have become close friends or colleagues with you, you should "break away" from them for a while so the new Company Commander has a fair chance to succeed. You can always continue those friendships and relationships later on down the road.

If you're considering resigning from the Army Reserve or Army National Guard, go out with a bang. Leave after you finish command. There's nothing like going out with a bang!

On the other hand, if you're considering making a long-term career out of the military, find a mentor to help you figure out what you need to do next.

I had several jobs after Company Command. I enjoyed them, but they didn't bring even 10% of the satisfaction that my time as a Company Commander did.

That's something you might struggle with too. But it's also something that you have to accept and learn to deal with. Most future jobs will be staff jobs and will have little troop involvement.

Conclusion

In conclusion, serving as a part-time Company Commander in the National Guard or Army Reserve is a unique, challenging, and rewarding experience.

Leading a group of Citizen-Soldiers, all while maintaining a family life, personal life and civilian career is extremely challenging and hard to do.

It takes someone with guts, hard-work, courage, tenacity and strong leadership skills to get the job done right. I know that you are up to the challenge. I encourage you to take the guidon, give it your best and never look back.

Although you will make many personal sacrifices to accomplish your mission, you will one day look back at your time in Company Command and realize that "it was worth it." All of the sacrifices you made were worth the memories and moments you experienced.

There is no greater honor than leading soldiers. Thanks for your service. Good luck in command!

About the Author

MAJ Holmes (former) was commissioned as an Active Duty Second Lieutenant in the Quartermaster Corps in May 2000.

He attended the Clarkson University R.O.T.C. Program and graduated from SUNY Potsdam, in upstate New York.

Prior to his commissioning, he was an Active Duty Enlisted Soldier in *The Old Guard*.

MAJ Holmes held a variety of positions on Active Duty and in the Army National Guard to include: Platoon Leader, Battalion S4, Company XO, Shop Officer, G4 Plans Officer, SSA Accountable Officer, Fuel Officer, Company Commander, Regimental S4 and Regimental S3 Officer.

Chuck served in the Maryland Army National Guard from 2005 to 2011. He deployed in support of Operation Iraqi Freedom (Iraq) and Operation Enduring Freedom (Kosovo).

He resigned from the IRR in April 2012. He is now a civilian. As a civilian, he is an author, blogger and network marketer.

He holds a Bachelor's Degree in Politics from SUNY Potsdam and a Master's in Management from Troy University. He is also a Certified Small Business Coach.

Chuck's hobbies include writing, reading, blogging, public speaking, network marketing, running, selling on eBay, food, family and funny movies.

Chuck lives in Homosassa, Florida with his wife Rachel. He makes his full-time living through his books and websites.

If you would like to connect with him, you can call him at (352) 503-4816 EST during business hours or send him an email to **chuck@part-time-commander.com**.

Recommended Reading List

Here is a short list of books I believe all Company Commanders should read. They are listed in alphabetical order.

Company Command: The Bottom Line by John G. Meyer

Developing the Leaders Around You: How to Help Others Reach their Full Potential by John C. Maxwell

First, Break all the Rules: What the World's Greatest Managers Do Differently by Marcus Buckingham

Good to Great: Why Some Companies Make the Leap... And Others Don't by Jim Collins

How to Win Friends and Influence People by Dale Carnegie

Leadership and the One Minute Manager: Increasing Effectiveness through Situational Leadership by Ken Blanchard

Now, Discover Your Strengths by Marcus Buckingham

Personality Plus: How to Understand Others by Understanding Yourself by Florence Littauer

Small Unit Leadership: A Common Sense Approach by Dandridge M. Malone

Taking the Guidon: Exceptional Leadership at the Company Level by Nate Allen and Tony Burgess

The Go-Getter: A Story that Tells You How to Be One by Peter Kyne

<u>The Magic of Thinking Big</u> by Dr. David Schwartz

<u>The One Minute Manager</u> by Ken Blanchard

<u>The 21 Irrefutable Laws of Leadership: Follow Them and People Will Follow You</u> by John C. Maxwell

<u>Who Moved My Cheese</u>? An Amazing Way to Deal with Change in Your Work and In Your Life by Spencer Johnson

To get a more comprehensive list, or to order some of these titles, visit our website at:

http://www.part-time-commander.com/reading-list/

Company Commander Training Course

I hope you enjoyed this book. If you are looking for additional training to help you become a successful Company Commander, I highly suggest you check out my *Company Commander Training Course*.

The *Company Commander Training Course* is a home study audio program on CDs for Company Commanders in the Army National Guard and Army Reserve.

To learn more visit my website at:

http://www.part-time-commander.com/company-commander-training-course/

Visit Our Website

If you enjoyed this book and are looking for more information about any of the following topics, please visit our website.

- Personal & Professional Development
- Career Tips
- Leadership Training
- How to Be Better at Your Job
- How to Develop Your Subordinates
- How to Get Promoted
- How to Get the Jobs You Want
- Or Anything Else!

We provide advice for officers, NCOs, soldiers, veterans and family members. We have nearly 1,500 different articles to help you advance your part-time military career.

www.Part-Time-Commander.com

Made in the USA
Middletown, DE
01 September 2019